Prentice Hall ASE Test Preparation Series

Steering and Suspension (A4)

James D. Halderman, Professor
Sinclair Community College
Dayton, Ohio
ASE Certified Master Automobile Technician
ASE Certified Advanced Level (L1)
ASE Certified Undercar Specialist
ASE Certified Master Engine Machinist

Chase D. Mitchell, Jr.
Utah Valley State College
Orem, Utah
ASE Certified Master Automobile Technician
ASE Certified Advanced Level (L1)

PEARSON

Prentice Hall

Upper Saddle River, New Jersey
Columbus, Ohio

D1262453

Editor in Chief: Stephen Helba
Executive Editor: Ed Francis
Production Editor: Christine M. Buckendahl
Design Coordinator: Diane Ernsberger
Cover Designer: Jeff Vanik
Production Manager: Brian Fox
Marketing Manager: Mark Marsden

This book was printed and bound by Courier Kendallville. The cover was printed by Phoenix Color Corp.

Pearson Education Ltd.
Pearson Education Australia Pty. Limited
Pearson Education Singapore Pte. Ltd.
Pearson Education North Asia Ltd.
Pearson Education Canada, Ltd.
Pearson Educación de Mexico, S.A. de C.V.
Pearson Education—Japan
Pearson Education Malaysia Pte. Ltd.
Pearson Education, *Upper Saddle River, New Jersey*

10 9 8 7 6 5 4 3 2 1
ISBN: 0-13-019194-9

Table of Contents

Preface

This study guide was written to help service technicians and students of automotive technology prepare to take the National ASE Certification Tests. This study guide includes the following features:

- **Sample ASE-type test questions** organized and correlated to the ASE test task list

- **Answers with detailed explanations** of why the right answer is correct as well as why the wrong answers are not correct

- **Heavily-illustrated questions and explanations** which explain the questions and answers.

- **A CD ROM** that includes additional study questions with answers plus additional study material to help the reader gain the knowledge necessary to successfully pass the ASE Certification Test

- **A coupon for FREE access to a Web site** for additional test questions that are graded online as you complete each 10-question quiz

- **A comprehensive English and Spanish language glossary** that gives detailed definitions of all technical words and terms used in the ASE Certification Test

- **Two appendixes** that address ASE assumed knowledge of environmental/ hazardous material handling and safety issues.

- **An index** allowing key words or topics to be quickly located.

About the ASE Tests

What is ASE?

ASE is an abbreviation for the **National Institute for Automotive Service Excellence** (simply known as ASE), which was formed in 1972 to provide standardized testing of service technicians.

ASE is a nonprofit association, and its main goal is to improve the quality of vehicle service through testing and volunteer certification.

What areas of vehicle service are covered by the ASE tests?

Automobile test service areas include:

- **A1** Engine Repair
- **A2** Automatic Transmission/Transaxle
- **A3** Manual Drive Train and Axles
- **A4** Suspension and Steering
- **A5** Brakes
- **A6** Electrical/Electronic Systems
- **A7** Heating and Air Conditioning
- **A8** Engine Performance

If a technician takes and passes all eight of the automobile tests and has achieved two or more years of work experience, ASE will award the designation of **ASE Certified Master Automobile Technician.** Contact ASE for other certification areas.

How can I contact ASE?

ASE
101 Blue Seal Drive, SE
Suite 101
Leesburg, VA 20175

Toll free: 1-877-ASE-TECH (273-8324)
1-703-669-6600
Web site: www.asecert.org

When are the tests given and where?

The ASE tests are given at hundreds of test sites in early May and early November of each year. Deadline for registration is usually in late March for the May tests and in late September for the November tests. Consult the ASE registration booklet or Web site for details and locations of the test sites.

What do I have to do to register?

You can register for the ASE tests in three ways:

1. Mail in the registration form that is in the registration booklet.
2. Register online at www.asecert.org.
3. Telephone at (703) 669-6600

Call ASE toll-free at 1-877-273-8324 or visit the Web site for details about cost and dates.

How many years of work experience are needed?

ASE requires that you have two or more years of full-time, hands-on working experience either as an automobile, truck, truck equipment, or school bus technician, engine machinist, or in collision repair, refinishing, or damage analysis and estimating for certification, except as noted below. If you have *not* previously provided work experience information, you will receive a Work Experience Report Form with your admission ticket. You *must* complete and return this form to receive a certificate.

Substitutions for work experience. You may receive credit for up to one year of the two-year work experience requirement by substituting relevant formal training in one, or a combination, of the following:

High School Training: Three full years of training, either in automobile/truck/school bus repair or in collision repair, refinishing, or damage estimating, may be substituted for one year of work experience.

Post-High School Training: Two full years of post-high school training in a public or private trade school, technical institute, community or four-year college, or in an apprenticeship program may be counted as one year of work experience.

Short Courses: For shorter periods of post-high school training, you may substitute two   months of training for one month of work experience.

You may receive full credit for the two-year work experience requirement with the following:

Completion of Apprenticeship: Satisfactory completion of either a three-or-four-year bona fide apprenticeship program.

Are there any hands-on activities on the ASE test?

No. All ASE tests are written using objective-type questions, meaning that you must select the correct answer from four possible alternatives.

Who writes the ASE questions?

All ASE test questions are written by a panel of industry experts, educators, and experienced ASE certified service technicians. Each question is reviewed by the committee and it is checked for the following:

- **Technically accurate.** All test questions use the correct terms and only test for vehicle manufacturer's recommended service procedures. Slang is not used nor are any aftermarket accessories included on the ASE test.

- **Manufacturer neutral.** All efforts are made to avoid using vehicle or procedures that are manufacturer specific such as to General Motors vehicles or to Toyotas. A service technician should feel comfortable about being able to answer the questions regardless of the type or brand of vehicle.

- **Logical answers.** All effort is made to be sure that all answers (not just the correct answers) are possible. While this may seem to make the test tricky, it is designed to test for real knowledge of the subject.

- **Random answer.** All efforts are made to be sure that the correct answers are not always the longest answer or that one letter, such as **c**, is not used more than any other letter.

What types of questions are asked on the ASE test?

All ASE test questions are objective. This means that there will not be questions where you will have to write an answer. Instead, all you have to do is select one of the four possible answers and place a mark in the correct place on the score sheet.

- **Multiple-choice questions**

  This type of question has one correct (or mostly correct) answer (called the key) and three incorrect answers (called distracters). A multiple-choice question example:

  What part of an automotive engine does not move?

  - a. Piston
  - b. Connecting rod
  - c. Block
  - d. Valve

  The correct answer is **c** (block). This type of question asks for a specific answer. Answer **a** (piston), **b** (connecting rod), and **d** (valve) all move during normal engine operation. The best answer is **c** (block) because even though it may vibrate, it does not move as the other parts do.

4

- **Technician A and Technician B questions**

  This type of question is generally considered to be the most difficult according to service technicians who take the ASE test. A situation or condition is usually stated and two technicians (A and B) say what they think could be the correct answer and you must decide which technician is correct.

  - a. Technician A only
  - b. Technician B only
  - c. Both Technicians A and B
  - d. Neither Technician A nor B

  The best way to answer this type of question is to carefully read the question and consider Technician A and Technician B answers to be solutions to a true or false question. If Technician A is correct, mark on the test by Technician A the letter T for true. (Yes, you can write on the test.) If Technician B is also correct, write the letter T for true by Technician B. Then mark **c** on your test score sheet, for both technicians are correct.

  Example:

  Two technicians are discussing an engine that has lower than specified fuel pressure. Technician A says that the fuel pump could be the cause. Technician B says that the fuel pressure regulator could be the cause.

  Which technician is correct?

  - a. Technician A only
  - b. Technician B only
  - **c. Both Technicians A and B**
  - d. Neither Technician A nor B

Analysis:

> Is Technician A correct? The answer is yes because if the fuel pump was defective, the pump pressure could be lower than specified by the vehicle manufacturer. Is Technician B correct? The answer is yes because a stuck open or a regulator with a weak spring could be the cause of lower than specified fuel pressure. The correct answer is therefore **c** (Both Technicians A and B are correct).

- **Most-likely-type questions**

This type of question asks which of the four possible items listed is the most likely to cause the problem or symptom. This type of question is often considered to be difficult because recent experience may lead you to answer the question incorrectly because even though it is possible, it is not the "most likely."

Example:

> Which of the items below is the most likely to cause blue exhaust at engine start?
>
> **a. Valve stem seals**
> b. Piston rings
> c. Clogged PCV valve
> d. A stuck oil pump regulator valve

Analysis:

> The correct answer is **a** because valve stem seals are the most likely to cause this problem. Answer **b** is not correct because even though worn piston rings can cause the engine to burn oil and produce blue exhaust smoke, it is not the most likely cause of blue smoke at engine start. Answers **c** and **d** are not correct because even though these items could contribute to the engine burning oil and producing blue exhaust smoke, they are not the most likely.

- **Except-type questions**

ASE will sometimes use a question that includes answers that are all correct except one. You have to determine which of the four questions is not correct.

Example:

A radiator is being pressure tested using a hand-operated tester. This test will check for leaks in all except:

a. Radiator
b. Heater core
c. Water pump
d. Evaporator

Analysis:

The correct answer is **d** because the evaporator is not included in the cooling system and will not be pressurized during this test. Answers **a** (radiator), **b** (heater core), and **c** (water pump) are all being tested under pressure exerted on the cooling system by the pressure tester.

- **Least-likely-type questions**

Another type of question asked on many ASE tests is a question that asks which of the following is least likely to be the cause of a problem or symptom. In other words, all of the answers are possible, but it is up to the reader to determine which answer is the least likely to be correct.

Example:

Which of the following is the least likely cause of low oil pressure?

a. Clogged oil pump screen
b. Worn main bearing
c. Worn camshaft bearing
d. Worn oil pump

Analysis:

The correct answer is **c** because even though worn camshaft bearings can cause low oil pressure, the other answers are more likely to be the cause.

Should I guess if I don't know the answer?

Yes. ASE tests simply record the correct answers, and by guessing, you will have at least a 25% (1 out of 4) chance. If you leave the answer blank, it will be scored as being incorrect. Instead of guessing entirely, try to eliminate as many of the answers as possible as not being very likely. If you can eliminate two out of the four, you have increased your chance of guessing to 50% (two out of four).

HINT: Never change an answer. Some research has shown that your first answer is most likely to be correct. It is human nature to read too much into the question rather than accept the question as it was written.

Is each test the same every time I take it?

No. ASE writes many questions for each area and selects from this "test bank" for each test session. You may see some of the same questions if you take the same test in the spring and then again in the fall, but you will also see many different questions.

Can I write or draw on the test form?

Yes. You may write or figure on the test, but do not write on the answer form or it can be misread during scanning and affect your score. You turn in your test and the answer form at the end of the session and the test is not reused.

Can I skip questions I don't know and come back to answer later?

Yes. You may skip a question if you wish, but be sure to mark the question and return to answer the question later. It is often recommended to answer the question or guess and go on with the test so that you do not run out of time to go back over the questions.

How much time do I have to take the tests?

All ASE test sessions are 4 hours and 15 minutes long. This is usually enough time for you to take up to four certification tests. ASE recommends that you do not attempt to take more than 225 questions or four tests at any one session. The ASE tests are spread over four days so it is possible to take all eight ASE test areas during a test period (spring or fall).

Will I have to know specifications and gauge readings?

Yes and no. You will be asked the correct range for a particular component or operation and you must know about what the specification should be. Otherwise, the questions will state that the value is less than or greater than the allowable specification. The question will deal with how the service technician should proceed or what action should be taken.

Can I take a break during the test?

Yes, you may use the restroom after receiving permission from the proctor of the test site.

Can I leave early if I have completed the test(s)?

Yes, you may leave quietly after you have completed the test(s). You must return the score sheet(s) and the test booklets as you leave.

How are the tests scored?

The ASE tests are machine scored and the results tabulated by American College Testing (ACT).

What percentage do I need to achieve to pass the ASE test?

While there is no exact number of questions that must be answered correctly in each area, an analysis of the test results indicate that the percentage needed to pass varies from 61% to 69%. Therefore, in order to pass the Suspension and Steering (A4) ASE certification test, you will have to answer about 26 questions correct out of 40. In other words, you can miss about 14 questions and still pass.

What happens if I do not pass? Do I have to wait a year before trying again?

No. If you fail to achieve a passing score on any ASE test, you can take the test again at the next testing session (in May or November).

Do I have to pay another registration fee if I already paid it once?

Yes. The registration fee is due at every test session in May or November whether you select to take one or more ASE tests. Therefore, it is wise to take as many tests as you can at each test session.

How long do I have to wait to know the results?

You will receive written notice within two months after the test. Notification is sent out in July for the May test and in January for the November test sessions. You will be notified that you either "passed" a test(s) or that "more preparation is needed," meaning that you did not score high enough to pass the test and be rewarded with certification in the content area.

Will I receive notice of which questions I missed?

ASE sends out a summary of your test results, which shows how many questions you missed in each category, but not individual questions.

Will ASE send me the correct answers to the questions I missed so I will know how to answer them in the future?

No. ASE will not send you the answers to test questions.

Are the questions in this study guide actual ASE test questions?

No. The test questions on the actual ASE certification tests are copyrighted and cannot be used by others. The test questions in this study guide cover the same technical information and the question format is similar to the style used on the actual test.

Test Taking Tips

Start Now

Even if you have been working on vehicles for a long time, taking an ASE certification test can be difficult. The questions will not include how things work or other "textbook" knowledge. The questions are based on "real world" diagnosis and service. The tests may seem tricky to some because the "distracters" (the wrong answers) are designed to be similar to the correct answer.

If this is your first time taking the test or you are going to recertify, start now to prepare. Allocate time each day to study.

Practice Is Important

Many service technicians do not like taking tests. As a result, many technicians rush through the test to get the pain over with quickly. Also, many service technicians have lots of experiences on many different vehicles. This is what makes them good at what they do, but when an everyday problem is put into a question format (multiple choice), the answer may not be as clear as your experience has taught you.

Keys to Success

The key to successful test taking includes:

- Practice answering similar type questions.
- Carefully read each question two times to make sure you understand the question.
- Read each answer.
- Pick the best answer.
- Avoid reading too much into each question.
- Do not change an answer unless you are sure that the answer is definitely wrong.
- Look over the glossary of automotive terms for words that are not familiar to you.

The best preparation is practice, practice, and more practice. This is where using the ASE Test Prep practice tests can help.

Prepare Mentally

Practicing also helps relieve another potential problem many people have called "chronic test syndrome." This condition is basically an inability to concentrate or focus during a test. The slightest noise, fear of failure, and worries about other things all contribute. The best medicine is practice, practice, and more practice. With practice, test taking becomes almost second nature.

Prepare Physically

Be prepared physically. Get enough sleep and eat right.

One Month Before the Test

- Budget your time for studying. On average you will need 4 to 6 hours of study for each test that you are taking.
- Use the ASE Test Prep Online test preparation service three or more times a week for your practice.
- Study with a friend or a group if possible.

The Week Before the Test

- Studying should consist of about 2 hours of reviewing for each test being taken.
- Make sure you know how to get to the testing center. If possible drive to the test site and locate the room.
- Get plenty of rest.

The Day of the Test

- Study time is over.
- Keep your work schedule light or get the day off if possible.
- Eat a small light meal the evening of the test.
- Drink a large glass of water 1 to 2 hours before the test. (The brain and body work on electrical impulses, and water is used as a conductor.)
- Arrive at least 30 minutes early at the test center. Be ready to start on time.

What to Bring to the Test

- A photo ID.
- Your Entry Ticket that came with your ASE packet.
- Two sharpened #2 pencils.

During the Test

- BREATHE (oxygen is the most important nutrient for the brain.)
- Read every question TWICE.
- Read ALL the ANSWERS.
- If you have trouble with a question, leave it blank and continue. At the end of the test, go back and try any skipped questions. (Frequently, you will get a hint in another question that follows.)

Study Guide and ASE Test Correlation Chart

This ASE study guide is divided into the sub-content areas that correlate to the actual ASE certification test as follows:

Test Area Covered	Number of ASE Certification Test Questions	Number of Study Guide Questions
Suspension and Steering (A4)	**40 total**	**103 total**
A. Steering Systems Diagnosis and Repair	10	28 (#1-#28*)
B. Suspension Systems Diagnosis and Repair	13	30 (#29-#58)
C. Wheel Alignment Diagnosis, Adjustment, and Repair	12	33 (#59-#91)
D. Wheel and Tire Diagnosis and Repair	5	12 (#92-#103)

*The study guide questions are numbered consecutively to make it easier to locate the correct answers in the back of the book.

Suspension and Steering (A4)

A. Steering Systems Diagnosis and Repair Questions

1. A "dry park" test to determine the condition of the steering components and joints should be performed with the vehicle _____.

   a. On level ground
   b. On turn plates that allow the front wheels to move
   c. On a frame contact lift with the wheels off the ground
   d. Lifted off the ground about 2 inches (5 cm)

2. Two technicians are discussing bump steer. Technician A says that an unlevel steering linkage can be the cause. Technician B says that if the steering wheel moves when the vehicle is bounced up and down, then the steering linkage may be bent. Which technician is correct?

   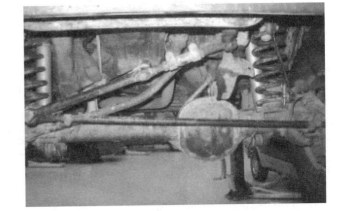

   a. Technician A only
   b. Technician B only
   c. Both Technicians A and B
   d. Neither Technician A nor B

3. Two technicians are discussing the proper procedure for bleeding air from a power steering system. Technician A says that the front wheels of the vehicle should be lifted off the ground before bleeding. Technician B says that the steering wheel should be turned left and right during the procedure. Which technician is correct?

   a. Technician A only
   b. Technician B only
   c. Both Technicians A and B
   d. Neither Technician A nor B

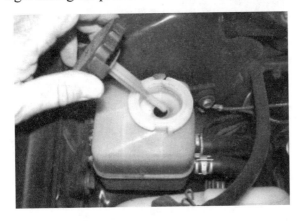

4. A power steering pressure test is being performed; the pressure is higher than specifications with the engine running and the steering wheel is stationary and in the straight-ahead position. Technician A says that a restricted high-pressure line could be the cause. Technician B says that internal leakage inside the steering gear or rack-and-pinion unit could be the cause. Which technician is correct?

    a. Technician A only
    b. Technician B only
    c. Both Technicians A and B
    d. Neither Technician A nor B

5. Two technicians are discussing the replacement of an inner tie rod end (ball-socket assembly) of a rack-and-pinion steering gear. Technician A says that the inner and outer tie rod ends are part of the rack and cannot be replaced separately. Technician B says that the steering gear unit should be removed from the vehicle before the inner tie rod end can be removed. Which technician is correct?

    a. Technician A only
    b. Technician B only
    c. Both Technicians A and B
    d. Neither Technician A nor B

6. Two technicians are discussing replacement of a tie rod end to the steering knuckle. Technician A says to tighten the nut to specifications and loosen slightly, if necessary, to align the cotter key. Technician B says to tighten the nut tighter if necessary if the cotter keyhole does not line up. Which technician is correct?

    a. Technician A only
    b. Technician B only
    c. Both Technicians A and B
    d. Neither Technician A nor B

7. What is adjustable with the adjustment slots for the idler arm?

    a. Play in the steering wheel
    b. Steering effort
    c. Steering wheel return after cornering
    d. Level steering linkage to prevent bump steer

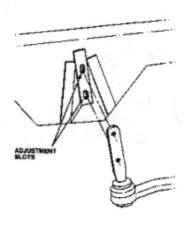

ADJUSTMENT SLOTS

8. Excessive steering wheel free play is being discussed. Technician A says that a worn steering flexible coupler could be the cause. Technician B says that a worn groove in the housing around the control valve could be the cause. Which technician is correct?

    a. Technician A only
    b. Technician B only
    c. Both Technicians A and B
    d. Neither Technician A nor B

9. Two technicians are discussing replacement of the pitman shaft seal on an integral power steering gear. Technician A says that the pitman arm must be removed before the old seal can be removed. Technician B says that the steering gear unit should be removed from the vehicle before the seal can be removed. Which technician is correct?

    a. Technician A only
    b. Technician B only
    c. Both Technicians A and B
    d. Neither Technician A nor B

10. A customer complains that the steering lacks power assist only when cold. Technician A says that the power steering fluid may be low. Technician B says that a worn housing around the rotary (spool) valve is the most likely cause. Which technician is correct?

    a. Technician A only
    b. Technician B only
    c. Both Technicians A and B
    d. Neither Technician A nor B

11. When replacing a rubber-bonded socket (RBS) tie rod end, the technician should be sure to

    a. Remove the original using a special tool
    b. Install and tighten the replacement with the front wheels in the straight-ahead position
    c. Grease the joint before installing on the vehicle
    d. Install the replacement using a special clamp vise

12. A driver complains that the vehicle darts or moves first toward one side and then to the other side of the road. Technician A says that bump steer caused by an unlevel steering linkage could be the cause. Technician B says that worn rack bushings could be the cause. Which technician is correct?

    a. Technician A only
    b. Technician B only
    c. Both Technicians A and B
    d. Neither Technician A nor B

13. The adjustment procedure for a typical integral power steering gear is _____.

    a. Over-center adjustment, then worm thrust bearing preload
    b. Worm thrust bearing preload, then the over-center adjustment
    c. Torque pitman arm retaining bolt, then the over-center adjustment
    d. Tie rod end, then worm thrust bearing preload

14. Technician A says the tie rod sleeve clamps should be positioned as shown on the left. Technician B says they should be installed as shown on the right. Which technician is correct?

    a. Technician A only
    b. Technician B only
    c. Both Technicians A and B
    d. Neither Technician A nor B

15. All of the following components can cause excessive play in the steering wheel *except:*

    a. A worn U-joint between the steering gear and the steering column shaft
    b. A worn outer tie rod end
    c. Loosened steering gear attachment bolts
    d. Over tightened center link retaining nuts

16. A power steering pressure gauge is being used to help diagnose the cause of hard steering. Technician A says that the pressure should be greater than 200 psi with the wheels straight ahead. Technician B says that pressure reaches its maximum reading when the wheels are turned against the stops. Which technician is correct?

    a. Technician A only
    b. Technician B only
    c. Both Technicians A and B
    d. Neither Technician A nor B

17. A customer complains that power steering assist stops when driving in the rain. What is the *most likely* cause?

    a. The steering linkage tie rod ends are getting wet causing a bind
    b. Water is getting into the power steering fluid through the high-pressure hose
    c. Moisture is getting into the steering gears displacing the lubricant
    d. The power steering pump drive belt is loose or defective

18. A tie rod end is being replaced. Technician A says the steering wheel may be crooked when driving straight and excessive tire wear can occur if an alignment is not performed. Technician B says that the power steering system should be bled after the tie rod is installed. Which technician is correct?

    a. Technician A only
    b. Technician B only
    c. Both Technicians A and B
    d. Neither Technician A nor B

19. A power steering pump is being tested using a pressure gauge. The pressure increases to the specified value when the valve is closed restricting the flow of fluid to the steering gear. The pressure only rises a little when the steering wheel is turned all the way to the left or right with the valve open. Technician A says the pump is weak and should be replaced. Technician B says the steering gear is defective and should be replaced. Which technician is correct?

    a. Technician A only
    b. Technician B only
    c. Both Technicians A and B
    d. Neither Technician A nor B

20. Which of the following is the *least likely* to cause loose steering?

    a. A loose pitman arm retaining nut
    b. A worn idler arm
    c. A worn center link
    d. A loose tie rod end

21. Power steering fluid is observed dripping out of the boots of the power rack and pinion steering gear assembly. What is the *most likely* cause?

    a. A loose or worn inner tire rod end (ball-socket assembly)
    b. Leaking control valve seals
    c. A leaking inner rack seal
    d. A loose stub U-joint

22. Two technicians are discussing airbags. Technician A says the airbag should be disabled when service work is going to be performed on the steering column or related components. Technician B says that the connector(s) for the airbags are yellow. Which technician is correct?

    a. Technician A only
    b. Technician B only
    c. Both Technicians A and B
    d. Neither Technician A nor B

23. A customer complains that the steering on a vehicle equipped with a conventional steering gear binds at times. Which is the *least likely* cause?

    a. A loose power steering belt
    b. A defective intermediate shaft U-joint
    c. Loose tie rod ends
    d. A defective ball-joint(s)

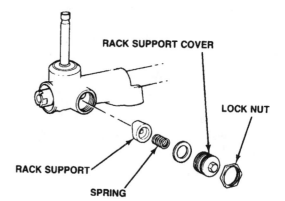

24. How should the rack support be adjusted?

    a. No adjustment necessary – just thread into the rack assembly
    b. Torque to 80 – 100 lb-ft
    c. Tighten and back off about 60°
    d. Tighten until all steering wheel free-play is eliminated

25. A defective upper strut mount can cause all of the following *except* _____.

    a. Binding
    b. Noise when driving over bumps
    c. Poor steering wheel return after turning a corner
    d. A crooked steering wheel

26. The power steering fluid is being checked on a vehicle equipped with a rack and pinion steering. The fluid is silver/black in color. Technician A says that this is normal for a vehicle equipped with rack and pinion steering. Technician B says the rack and pinion gear teeth must be worn because the silver color is likely a result of the wear metals. Which technician is correct?

    a. Technician A only
    b. Technician B only
    c. Both Technicians A and B
    d. Neither Technician A nor B

27. What is being measured in the illustration?

    a. The tie rod bending strength
    b. Free play of the inner ball socket assembly
    c. Toe-in
    d. The play in the tie rod

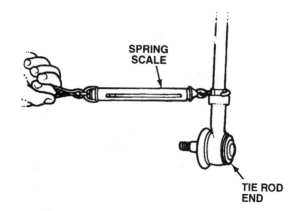

28. If this part were to fail, what would be the *most likely* symptom?

    a. Hard, stiff steering
    b. Excessive free-play in the steering wheel
    c. Shimmy-type vibration in the steering wheel at highway speeds
    d. Wandering when driving straight

Suspension and Steering (A4)

B. Suspension Systems Diagnosis and Repair Questions

29. A noise is heard from the front end of the vehicle while traveling over bumpy sections of road. Technician A says that worn or deteriorated control arm bushings could be the cause. Technician B says that worn or deteriorated strut rod bushings could be the cause. Which technician is correct?

    a. Technician A only
    b. Technician B only
    c. Both Technicians A and B
    d. Neither Technician A nor B

30. Two technicians are discussing the inspection of load-carrying ball joints. Technician A says that the vehicle should be on the ground with the ball joints *loaded*, then checked for free-play movement. Technician B says that the ball joints should be *unloaded* before checking for free-play in the ball joints. Which technician is correct?

    a. Technician A only
    b. Technician B only
    c. Both Technicians A and B
    d. Neither Technician A nor B

31. A light film of oil is observed on the upper area of a shock absorber. Technician A says that this condition should be considered normal. Technician B says that a rod seal may bleed fluid during cold weather causing the oil film. Which technician is correct?

    a. Technician A only
    b. Technician B only
    c. Both Technicians A and B
    d. Neither Technician A nor B

32. A vehicle equipped with coil-spring front suspension and a leaf-spring rear suspension "dog tracks" while driving on a straight, level road. Technician A says that a broken center bolt could be the cause. Technician B says defective upper control arm bushings on the front could be the cause. Which technician is correct?

    a. Technician A only
    b. Technician B only
    c. Both Technicians A and B
    d. Neither Technician A nor B

33. What part *must* be replaced when servicing the outer wheel bearing on a non-drive wheel?

    a. The bearing cup
    b. The grease seal
    c. The cotter key
    d. The retainer washer

34. A defective wheel bearing usually sounds like _____.

    a. Marbles in a tin can
    b. A noisy tire
    c. A baby rattle
    d. A clicking sound – like a ballpoint pen

35. Two technicians are discussing a vehicle that is sagging at the rear. Technician A says that new shock absorbers will restore the vehicle to proper ride height. Technician B says that the rear springs should be replaced. Which technician is correct?

    a. Technician A only
    b. Technician B only
    c. Both Technicians A and B
    d. Neither Technician A nor B

36. An indicator-type ball joint is shown. Technician A says that the ball joint is worn and should be replaced. Technician B says that the ball joint is serviceable. Which technician is correct?

    a. Technician A only
    b. Technician B only
    c. Both Technicians A and B
    d. Neither Technician A nor B

37. A fleet vehicle was found to have damaged suspension-limiting rubber bump stops (jounce bumpers). Technician A says sagging springs could be the cause. Technician B says defective or worn shock absorbers could be the cause. Which technician is correct?

    a. Technician A only
    b. Technician B only
    c. Both Technicians A and B
    d. Neither Technician A nor B

38. The preferred method to use to separate tapered chassis parts it to use a _____.

    a. Pickle fork tool
    b. Torch to heat the joint until it separates
    c. Puller tool
    d. Drill to drill out the tapered part

39. Before the strut cartridge can be removed from a typical MacPherson strut assembly, which operation is necessary to prevent possible personal injury?

    a. The brake caliper and/or brake hose should be removed from the strut housing
    b. The coil spring should be compressed
    c. The upper strut mounting bolts should be removed
    d. The lower attaching bolts should be removed

40. Two technicians are discussing wheel bearings that were discovered to have dents in the outer race (brinnelling). Technician A says the vehicle may have been overloaded. Technician B says that the bearing may have been over tightened. Which technician is correct?

    a. Technician A only
    b. Technician B only
    c. Both Technicians A and B
    d. Neither Technician A nor B

41. Technician A says that indicator ball joints should be loaded with the weight of the vehicle on the ground to observe the wear indicator. Technician B says that the nonindicator ball joints should be inspected *unloaded*. Which technician is correct?

    a. Technician A only
    b. Technician B only
    c. Both Technicians A and B
    d. Neither Technician A nor B

42. What is being done in the drawing?

    a. Replacing a control arm bushing
    b. Adjusting a ball-joint
    c. Replacing a ball joint
    d. Straightening a bent or damaged control arm

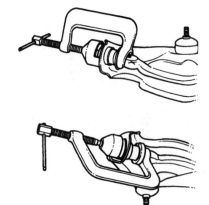

43. The axial play in a lower load-carrying ball joint is measured and it is 0.150 in. (3.8 mm). Technician A says the ball joint should be replaced. Technician B says that the lower ball joint on the other side of the vehicle should also be replaced. Which technician is correct?

    a. Technician A only
    b. Technician B only
    c. Both Technicians A and B
    d. Neither Technician A nor B

44. A rear-wheel-drive vehicle equipped with front coil springs and rear leaf springs is sagging down at the right rear and the left front is higher than the right front. Which is the *most likely* cause?

    a. A broken stabilizer bar link in the left front
    b. A broken rear track rod
    c. A broken leaf spring on the right rear
    d. A broken left front shock absorber

45. A pull toward one side during braking is one symptom of defective or worn _____.

    a. Stabilizer bar links
    b. Strut rod bushings
    c. Rear leaf springs
    d. Track (panhard) rod

46. Two technicians are discussing the installation of a replacement strut cartridge. Technician A says that about 1 ounce of engine oil should be installed in the strut housing before inserting the cartridge. Technician B says that the strut cartridge itself has to be filled with oil. Which technician is correct?

    a. Technician A only
    b. Technician B only
    c. Both Technicians A and B
    d. Neither Technician A nor B

47. If the rear track rod (panhard rod) is bent, what problem is the *most likely* to occur?

    a. The vehicle will sway when rounding curves
    b. The rear axle will be out of alignment with the front wheels
    c. A loud knocking noise will be heard during turns
    d. The vehicle pulls to one side during braking

48. Both holes in the lower control arms as shown are covered by the coil spring. Technician A says that the spring may be installed upside down. Technician B says the spring is installed correctly. Which technician is correct?

    a. Technician A only
    b. Technician B only
    c. Both Technicians A and B
    d. Neither Technician A nor B

49. A vehicle wanders when traveling at highway speeds and the driver has to make constant corrections to the steering wheel to maintain control. Which is the *least likely* to cause this problem?

    a. Worn control arm bushings
    b. Worn ball joints
    c. Leaking shock absorbers/struts
    d. Worn strut rod bushings

50. The rear of a sport utility vehicle is sagging. Which is the *least likely* cause?

    a. Excessive load in the rear of the vehicle
    b. Incorrect springs
    c. Broken spring seats
    d. Leaking shock absorbers

51. One rear leaf spring is broken on a rear-wheel-drive vehicle. Technician A says that both rear springs should be replaced. Technician B says that rear shock absorbers may have to be replaced to restore proper ride height. Which technician is correct?

    a. Technician A only
    b. Technician B only
    c. Both Technicians A and B
    d. Neither Technician A nor B

52. What is the *most likely* cause of this condition on the rear of this front-wheel-drive vehicle?

    a. Excessively worn stabilizer bar bushings
    b. A broken rear track rod
    c. A broken rear control arm or ball joint
    d. A broken shock absorber

53. A vehicle makes a loud clunking sound only when the brakes are applied. Which is the *most likely* cause?

    a. A worn or defective strut rod (compression/tension) bushing
    b. A worn shock absorber
    c. Sagging springs
    d. A loose wheel bearing

54. A noisy rear suspension is being diagnosed. Technician A says that sagging rear springs can be the cause. Technician B says that damaged or missing spring insulators could be the cause. Which technician is correct?

    a. Technician A only
    b. Technician B only
    c. Both Technicians A and B
    d. Neither Technician A nor B

55. A vehicle has ride (trim) height lower on the left side than on the right side. Which is the *most likely* cause?

    a. Worn ball joints on the left side
    b. A worn or leaking shock absorber on the right side
    c. A weak or leaking shock absorber on the left side
    d. Sagging springs on the left side

56. A rear-wheel-drive vehicle has been hoisted on a frame-type lift and the rear shock absorbers are being replaced. Technician A says that the rear axle should be supported to prevent it from falling when the rear shocks are removed. Technician B says the rear springs should be compressed before the shocks are removed. Which technician is correct?

    a. Technician A only
    b. Technician B only
    c. Both Technicians A and B
    d. Neither Technician A nor B

57. New front coil springs are being installed to correct a sag condition. Technician A says that the springs are often marked left and right and should be replaced on the specified side of the vehicle. Technician B says that the springs must be installed right side up to be sure that they fit correctly in the spring seats. Which technician is correct?

    a. Technician A only
    b. Technician B only
    c. Both Technicians A and B
    d. Neither Technician A nor B

58. A pickup truck with a twin-I beam front suspension is hoisted and the front tires angle outward at the top as shown. Technician A says that the camber needs to be changed. Technician B says this is normal when the front suspension is in full droop when hoisted on a frame control-type lift. Which technician is correct?

    a. Technician A only
    b. Technician B only
    c. Both Technicians A and B
    d. Neither Technician A nor B

Suspension and Steering (A4)

C. Wheel Alignment Diagnosis, Adjustment, and Repair Questions

59. Technician A says that a vehicle will pull (or lead) to the side with the most camber (or least negative camber) if the difference exceeds factory specifications. Technician B says that a vehicle will pull (or lead) to the side with the most front toe. Which technician is correct?

    a. Technician A only
    b. Technician B only
    c. Both Technicians A and B
    d. Neither Technician A nor B

60. Which angle will be changed by adjusting strut rods (if applicable)?

    a. Toe
    b. Camber
    c. Caster
    d. Toe-out on turns

61. A front-wheel-drive vehicle with independent rear suspension pulls to the right. Technician A says that the right rear could be toed in more than the left rear. Technician B says that incorrect front toe could be the cause. Which technician is correct?

    a. Technician A only
    b. Technician B only
    c. Both Technicians A and B
    d. Neither Technician A nor B

62. If metal shims are used for alignment adjustment in the front as shown, they adjust _____.

    a. Camber
    b. Caster
    c. Toe
    d. Camber and caster

63. A pickup truck was aligned and then the owner installed a heavy camper. Technician A says that the extra weight will change the camber and caster on the front wheel. Technician B says that the weight will cause the toe to change. Which technician is correct?

    a. Technician A only
    b. Technician B only
    c. Both Technicians A and B
    d. Neither Technician A nor B

USE THE FOLLOWING INFORMATION TO ANSWER QUESTION 64:

Specifications:	**Min.**	**Preferred**	**Max.**
Camber	0°	1.0°	1.4°
Caster	.8°	1.5 °	2.1°
Toe	0.10°	0.06°	0.15°

Results:	**L**	**R**
Camber	-0.1°	0.6°
Caster	1.8°	1.6°
Toe	-0.3°	+0.12°

64. The vehicle above will _____.

    a. Pull toward the right and feather edge both tires
    b. Pull toward the left
    c. Wear the outside of the left tire and the inside of the right tire
    d. Wear the inside of both front tires and pull to the left

USE THE FOLLOWING INFORMATION TO ANSWER QUESTIONS #65 AND #66:

Specifications:	**Min.**	**Preferred**	**Max.**
Camber	-0.25°	+0.5°	1°
Caster	0°	+2 °	+4°
Toe	0°	0.1°	0.2°

Results:	**L**	**R**
Camber	-0.2°	+0.1°
Caster	3.6°	1.8°
Toe	-0.16°	+0.32°

65. The vehicle above will _____.

    a. Pull toward the left
    b. Pull toward the right
    c. Wander
    d. Lead to the left slightly

66. The vehicle above will _____.

    a. Wander
    b. Wear tires, but will not pull
    c. Will pull, but not wear tires
    d. Pull toward the left and cause feather-edge tire wear

67. The right front tire is worn on the outside and the vehicle pulls toward the right. Technician A says that the camber on the right front may need to be adjusted. Technician B says that caster on the right front may need to be adjusted. Which technician is correct?

    a. Technician A only
    b. Technician B only
    c. Both Technicians A and B
    d. Neither Technician A nor B

68. Which alignment angle is most likely to need correction and cause the most tire wear?

    a. Toe
    b. Camber
    c. Caster
    d. SAI

69. A front-wheel-drive vehicle pulls toward the right during rapid acceleration from a stop. The most *likely cause* is _____.

    a. Worn or defective tires
    b. Leaking or defective shock absorbers
    c. Normal torque steer
    d. A defective power steering rack-and-pinion steering assembly

70. A vehicle is pulling to the right. Technician A says that more camber on the right than the left could be the cause. Technician B says that more toe-in on the left than on the right could be the cause. Which technician is correct?

    a. Technician A only
    b. Technician B only
    c. Both Technicians A and B
    d. Neither Technician A nor B

71. A vehicle pulls to the right after turning a right turn and pulls to the left after turning a left turn. Technician A says that the upper strut bearing could be the cause. Technician B says that excessive positive caster on both front wheels could be the problem. Which technician is correct?

    a. Technician A only
    b. Technician B only
    c. Both Technicians A and B
    d. Neither Technician A nor B

72. An owner wants to install larger wheels and tires on his sport utility vehicle (SUV). Technician A says that the camber and toe will change. Technician B says that the SAI and included angle will be changed if larger wheels and tires are installed. Which technician is correct?

    a. Technician A only
    b. Technician B only
    c. Both Technicians A and B
    d. Neither Technician A nor B

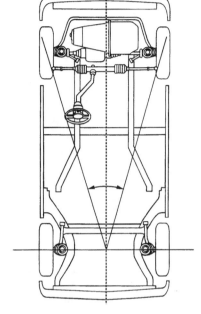

73. If the turning radius (toe-out on turns or Ackerman angle as shown) is out of specification, what should be replaced?

    a. The outer tie rod ends
    b. The inner tie rod ends
    c. The idler arm
    d. The steering knuckle

74. The thrust angle is being corrected. The alignment technician should adjust which angle to reduce thrust angle?

    a. Rear camber
    b. Front SAI or included angle and camber
    c. Rear toe
    d. Rear caster

75. A four-wheel alignment is being performed on a front-wheel-drive vehicle. The first angle corrected should be the _____.

    a. Front camber
    b. Front caster
    c. Rear toe
    d. Front toe

76. Adding a wedge as shown will change what angle in the rear of this front-wheel-drive vehicle?

    a. Rear camber
    b. Rear toe
    c. Rear caster
    d. Rear SAI

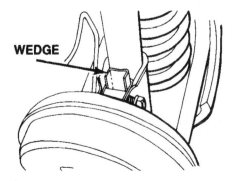

WEDGE

USE THE FOLLOWING SPECIFICATIONS TO ANSWER QUESTIONS #77 THROUGH #79:

front camber	$0.5° \pm 0.3°$
front caster	$3.5°$ to $4.5°$
toe	$0° \pm 0.1°$
rear camber	$0° \pm 0.5°$
rear toe	$-0.1°$ to $0.1°$

Alignment angles:

front camber left	$0.5°$	total toe	$0.0°$
front camber right	$-0.1°$	rear camber left	$0.15°$
front caster left	$3.8°$	rear camber right	$-0.11°$
front caster right	$4.5°$	rear toe left	$-0.04°$
front toe left	$-0.2°$	rear toe right	$0.08°$
front toe right	$+0.2°$		

77. Technician A says that the present alignment will cause excessive tire wear to the inside of both front tires. Technician B says the rear of the vehicle will dog track because of the difference in the rear toe. Which technician is correct?

    a. Technician A only
    b. Technician B only
    c. Both Technicians A and B
    d. Neither Technician A nor B

78. Technician A says the present alignment will cause excessive tire wear to the rear tires. Technician B says total front toe being set to zero will not cause any tire wear or handling concerns. Which technician is correct?

    a. Technician A only
    b. Technician B only
    c. Both Technicians A and B
    d. Neither Technician A nor B

79. With the present alignment, the vehicle will _____.

    a. Pull toward the right
    b. Go straight
    c. Pull toward the left
    d. Wander

80. Two technicians are discussing what could be causing a rear-wheel-drive vehicle to wander while driving straight on a level, straight road. Technician A says that low or unequal tire pressure could be the cause. Technician B says that loose or worn steering linkage could be the cause. Which technician is correct?

    a. Technician A only
    b. Technician B only
    c. Both Technicians A and B
    d. Neither Technician A nor B

81. A steering wheel is not straight when the vehicle is traveling on a straight highway. Which adjustment or procedure should the technician perform?

    a. Remove the steering wheel and reattach in the straight ahead position
    b. Adjust the camber angle
    c. Adjust the tie rod sleeves (toe angle)
    d. Adjust the caster angle

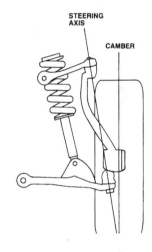

82. A front-wheel-drive vehicle equipped with a MacPherson strut front suspension is being checked for proper alignment. The SAI is OK, but the camber and included angle are less than specifications. What is the *most likely* cause?

    a. No problem – this is normal for a front-wheel-drive vehicle
    b. A worn ball joint(s)
    c. Worn tie rod ends
    d. A bent strut

83. A vehicle owner complains that the front tires squeal when turning a corner even at very low speeds. Which is the *most likely* cause?

    a. A bent center link
    b. A bent steering arm
    c. A loose idler arm
    d. Worn ball joints

84. A front-wheel-drive vehicle equipped with a MacPherson-type front suspension is being aligned. The left camber is –1.0° and the right camber is +1.0°. Technician A says the engine cradle could be shifted to the left. Technician B says that a leaking strut could be the cause. Which technician is correct?

    a. Technician A only
    b. Technician B only
    c. Both Technicians A and B
    d. Neither Technician A nor B

85. A front-wheel-drive vehicle with an independent rear suspension pulls to the right. Technician A says that unequal front toe can be the cause. Technician B says that unequal rear toe could be the cause. Which technician is correct?

    a. Technician A only
    b. Technician B only
    c. Both Technicians A and B
    d. Neither Technician A nor B

86. A customer is experiencing steering wheel up and down (tramp) vibration at highway speeds. Technician A says the front wheel camber could be out of specifications. Technician B says that the front toe may be out of specifications. Which technician is correct?

    a. Technician A only
    b. Technician B only
    c. Both Technicians A and B
    d. Neither Technician A nor B

87. Rotating the cam bolts will change _____.

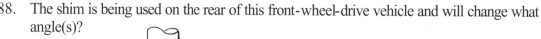

    a. Camber only
    b. Caster only
    c. Both camber and caster
    d. SAI

88. The shim is being used on the rear of this front-wheel-drive vehicle and will change what angle(s)?

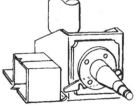

    a. Rear camber and toe
    b. Rear camber only
    c. Rear toe only
    d. Rear camber and caster

89. The eccentric cam is being rotated on the strut as shown, which will change what angle(s)?

    a. Caster
    b. Toe
    c. Camber
    d. SAI and caster

90. The camber needs to be increased (more positive) on the suspension shown without affecting the caster angle. Which of the following should be performed?

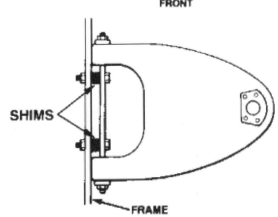

a. Add shims to the front only
b. Add equal shims to the front and rear
c. Move shim(s) from the front to the rear
d. Remove equal shims from the front and rear

91. Adjustment made at the exploded view component as shown would change which angle?

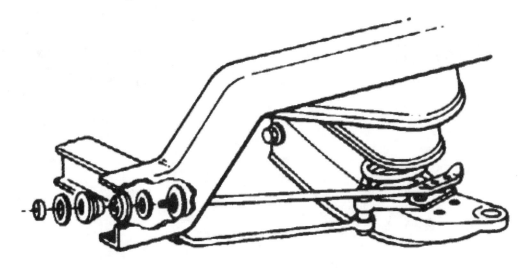

a. Camber
b. Caster
c. Toe
d. Toe-out on turns (TOOT)

Suspension and Steering (A4)

D. Wheel and Tire Diagnosis and Repair Questions

92. Using the modified X tire rotation method on a front-wheel drive vehicle would place the right front tire on the _____.

    a. Left front
    b. Left rear
    c. Right rear
    d. Right front

93. Most manufacturers of passenger vehicles specify a lug nut (wheel nut) tightening torque specification of about _____.

    a. 80 to 100 lb-ft
    b. 100 to 125 lb-ft
    c. 125 to 150 lb-ft
    d. 150 to 175 lb-ft

94. A tire is worn excessively on both edges. The most likely cause of this type of tire wear is _____.

    a. Over inflation
    b. Under inflation
    c. Excessive radial runout
    d. Excessive lateral runout

95. When seating a bead of a tire, never exceed _____ psi.

    a. 30 psi
    b. 40 psi
    c. 50 psi
    d. 60 psi

96. Which type of wheel weight should a technician use on aluminum (alloy) wheels?

    a. Lead with plated spring steel clips
    b. Coated (painted) lead weights
    c. Lead weights with longer than normal clips
    d. Aluminum weights

97. Technician A says that lug nuts should be tightened in a star pattern. Technician B says that a torque wrench should be used to be assured that all of the lug nuts are uniformly tightened and to the specified torque. Which technician is correct?

     a. Technician A only
     b. Technician B only
     c. Both Technicians A and B
     d. Neither Technician A nor B

98. Two technicians are discussing mounting a tire on a wheel. Technician A says that for best balance, the tire should be match mounted. Technician B says that silicone spray should be used to lubricate the tire bead. Which technician is correct?

     a. Technician A only
     b. Technician B only
     c. Both Technicians A and B
     d. Neither Technician A nor B

99. A tire has excessive radial runout. Technician A says that it should be broken down on a tire-changing machine and the tire rotated 180° on the wheel and retested. Technician B says that the tire should be replaced. Which technician is correct?

     a. Technician A only
     b. Technician B only
     c. Both Technicians A and B
     d. Neither Technician A nor B

100. Two technicians are discussing a vehicle that has excessive lateral runout. Technician A says the rim could be bent. Technician B says the hub could have excessive runout. Which technician is correct?

     a. Technician A only
     b. Technician B only
     c. Both Technicians A and B
     d. Neither Technician A nor B

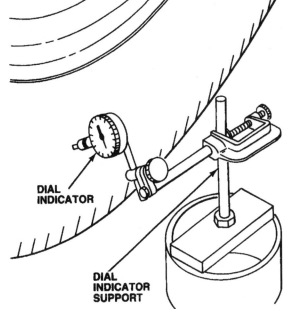

101. What is the *most likely* cause of this type of tire wear on the left rear of a front-wheel-drive vehicle?

    a. Incorrect rear toe
    b. Incorrect rear camber
    c. Over inflation
    d. Under inflation

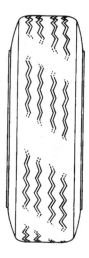

102. Wheels were installed on a vehicle using an air impact wrench without using a torque absorbing adapter. What would be the *most likely* to occur?

    a. Hard to remove
    b. No harm
    c. Vibration and possible warped rotors/drums
    d. Wheel/tire assembly out of balance

103. A rear-wheel drive vehicle has a vibration that is felt in the steering wheel at highway speeds. Technician A says that the drive shaft (prop shaft) may be bent or out of balance. Technician B says that the front tires could be out of balance. Which technician is correct?

    a. Technician A only
    b. Technician B only
    c. Both Technicians A and B
    d. Neither Technician A nor B

Suspension and Steering (A4)

A. Steering Systems Diagnosis and Repair Answers and Explanations

1. **The correct answer is a.** The vehicle must be on level ground when conducting a dry park; with the vehicle weight on the front wheels, resistance is applied to the steering linkage. Answers **b, c,** and **d** are not correct because these methods will allow the front wheels to move and not apply a load on the steering linkage.

2. **The correct answer is c.** Technician A is correct because unlevel steering linkage will cause a turning force to be applied to the front wheels when they move up and down during normal suspension movement. Technician B is correct because the steering linkage must be parallel to the suspension and move together to prevent suspension movement from affecting the steering. Answers **a, b,** and **d** are not correct because both technicians are correct.

3. **The correct answer is c.** Both technicians are correct. Technician A is correct because keeping the front wheels off the ground helps prevent any trapped air from dispersing into small bubbles or foam due to the resistance forces created by the weight of the vehicle on the ground. Technician B is correct because the steering wheel must be turned all the way to the left and all the way to the right to allow fluid to flow through the power steering system to allow any trapped air to escape. Answers **a, b,** and **d** are not correct because both technicians are correct.

4. **The correct answer is a.** Technician A is correct because pressure is created by a restriction and normal resistance in the steering gear would create normal pressure, whereas excessive pressure would be created by a restriction that is not normal in the system. Technician B is not correct because the pressure would be lower (not higher) if there was an internal leakage in the steering gear because normal restriction is being bypassed. Answers **c** and **d** are not correct because only Technician A is correct.

5. **The correct answer is d.** Neither technician is correct. Technician A is not correct because the inner tie-rod ends are separate components and can be replaced separately in most vehicles. Technician B is not correct because the inner tie-rod end can usually be replaced without requiring that the rack and pinion steering gear unit be removed. Answer **c** is not correct because neither technician is correct.

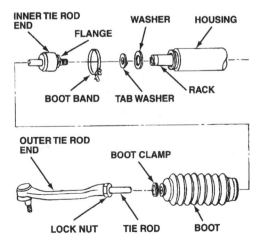

38

6. **The correct answer is b.** Technician B is correct because the nut retaining a tapered stud should never be loosened, but rather tightened further to align the cotter keyhole to prevent the joint from loosening. Technician A is not correct because the nut should be tightened and not loosened to align the cotter key to avoid the tapered part loosening. Answers **c** and **d** are not correct because Technician B only is correct.

7. **The correct answer is d.** Bump steer is caused by unlevel steering linkage, which causes a force to be applied to the steering linkage when the suspension moves up and down during normal driving. To achieve level steering linkage, some vehicles are equipped with adjustable slots that allow the idler arm to be moved up or down. Answers **a, b,** and **c** are not correct because the slots are used to adjust the idler arm to prevent bump steer and no other purpose.

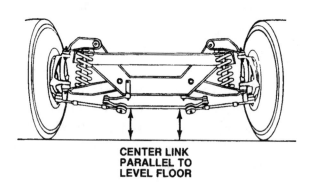

CENTER LINK PARALLEL TO LEVEL FLOOR

8. **The correct answer is a.** Technician A is correct because a worn flexible coupler located on the intermediate shaft of the steering column between the steering wheel and the steering gear can cause excessive steering wheel free play. Technician B is not correct because a worn groove in the control valve housing will not cause excessive steering wheel free play although it could cause hard steering when the vehicle is cold. Answers **c** and **d** are not correct because Technician A only is correct.

9. **The correct answer is d.** Neither technician is correct. Technician A is not correct because the pitman shaft seal can be replaced without removing the pitman shaft by removing the pitman arm retaining nut, pitman arm, and pitman seal retaining snap ring. Technician B is not correct because the steering gear does not *have* to be removed to replace the pitman seal. Answer **c** is not correct because neither technician is correct.

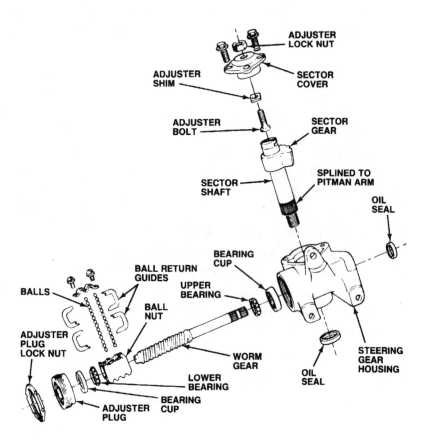

10. **The correct answer is b.** Technician B is correct because a worn control valve housing in the steering gear would allow power steering fluid to leak past the seals and result in hard steering until the fluid warms allowing the Teflon® seals to become pliable and begin to seal the fluid. Technician A is not correct because low power steering fluid is unlikely to cause a lack of power assist when cold only although it could cause excessive noise due to aeration of the fluid. Answers **c** and **d** are not correct because Technician B only is correct.

11. **The correct answer is b.** All steering components, especially those parts that use rubber-bonded socket (RBS) design, should be installed and tightened with the vehicle wheel in the straight ahead position. Rubber has a memory, and if the front wheels are turned when the parts are installed, the vehicle will likely pull in the direction the wheels were turned when the part(s) was installed. Answer **a** is not correct because a special tool beyond what would be necessary to service conventional steering components is not needed. Answer **c** is not correct because RBS components should not be greased as damage or deterioration of the rubber could result. Answer **d** is not correct because a special tool or holding fixture is not required to install a rubber bonded socket tie-rod end.

12. **The correct answer is c.** Both technicians are correct. Technician A is correct because if the steering linkage is not level, it will cause a force that steers the front wheels when the suspension moves up and down. Technician B is correct because worn or damaged rack bushings can cause the steering rack to tilt down at one end creating a bump steer condition. Answers **a, b,** and **d** are not correct because both technicians are correct.

13. **The correct answer is b.** The proper procedure to adjust a typical integral power steering gear is to adjust the worm gear thrust bearing preload, and then the over-center adjustment. Answers **a, c,** and **d** are not correct because they do not specify the correct adjustment procedure.

14. **The correct answer is a.** Technician A is correct because the clamp should cover the split on the tire rod adjusting sleeve. Technician B is not correct because the clamp and sleeve openings are aligned, which could reduce the clamping force on the sleeve. Answers **c** and **d** are not correct because only Technician A is correct.

15. **The correct answer is d.** An over tightened center link retaining nut is unlikely to cause excessive steering wheel play. Answers **a, b,** and **c** are all likely to cause excessive play in the steering wheel.

16. **The correct answer is b.** Technician B is correct because the steering gear provides a restriction to the flow of the power steering fluid when the steering wheel is turned all the way against the stop either to the left or to the right. Technician A is not correct because the steering gear presents little restriction with the wheels in the straight ahead position and should have less than 150 psi in the power steering system unless there is an unwanted restriction in the system. Answers **c** and **d** are not correct because only Technician B is correct.

17. **The correct answer is d.** A loose or worn power steering pump drive belt could cause a lack of power assist if covered with water reducing the ability of the belt to apply engine torque to the power steering pump. Answer **a** is not correct because water could not cause the tie rod to bind. Answer **b** is not likely because the power steering system is sealed and is unlikely to cause a lack of power assist if some water did get into the power steering pump reservoir. Answer **c** is not correct because the steering gear uses power steering fluid as a lubricant and as stated in answer **b**, is not likely to cause a lack of power assist.

18. **The correct answer is a.** Technician A is correct because replacing the tie rod end can affect the toe setting and cause the steering wheel to be crooked if an alignment is not performed after the repair. Excessive tire wear can also occur if the toe is not correct. Technician B is not correct because replacing the tie rod end would not cause air to get into the power steering hydraulic system. Answers **c** and **d** are not correct because only Technician A is correct.

19. **The correct answer is b.** Technician B is correct because the steering gear should restrict the flow of power steering fluid causing the pressure to increase as the front wheels are turned left and right. The pressure did increase when the valve was closed indicating that the pump is capable of supplying the necessary pressure, but the steering gear is leaking internally and requires repair or replacement. Technician A is not correct because the pump was capable of supplying the specified pressure when the valve was closed and is therefore, not at fault. Answers **c** and **d** are not correct because Technician B only is correct.

20. **The correct answer is a.** A loose pitman arm retaining nut is not likely to cause loose steering (excessive play in the steering wheel) because the pitman arm is splined to the pitman (sector) shaft and the nut is simply provided to keep the arm from falling off of the shaft. Answers **b, c,** and **d** are not correct because each can cause excessive play in the steering if worn.

21. **The correct answer is c.** A leaking inner rack seal will allow power steering fluid to leak into the rack housing and eventually drip from around the dust boots, which are designed to keep water and dirt from getting into the rack housing and are not designed to seal power steering fluid. Answer **a** is not correct because a loose or worn inner tie rod end boot will not cause a power steering fluid leak because the power steering fluid should be sealed by the inner and outer rack seals. Answer **b** is not correct because a leaking control valve seal will cause hard steering, especially when the vehicle is cold, but will not cause an external leak. Answer **d** is not correct because a loose stub shaft retaining nut could cause fluid leakage out of the top of a "hat" portion of the steering gear and not out of the boots.

22. **The correct answer is c.** Both technicians are correct. Technician A is correct because the airbags should be temporarily disabled when service work is being performed on or near the steering column to avoid the possibility of accidental deployment. Technician B is correct because all airbags (supplemental inflatable restraints) use yellow electrical connectors for easy identification. Answers **a, b,** and **d** are not correct because both technicians are correct.

23. **The correct answer is c.** Loose tie rod ends would be the least likely cause for the steering to bind at times because the steering would feel loose and have excessive play. Answer **a** is not correct because a loose power steering belt can cause the power steering pump to work some times and not work at other times creating a feeling that the steering is OK one instant and not working or binding another time. Answer **b** is not correct because a defective intermediate shaft U-joint can bind at times depending on the angle of the U-joint and how fast the steering wheel is turned. Answer **d** is not correct because a defective ball-joint can cause a bind if the internal parts rub without proper lubrication causing the front wheels to bind when being turned.

24. **The correct answer is c.** The rack support should be tightened and then backed off (rotated counterclockwise) 60° on one flat of the hex-shaped adjusting nut. Answer **a** is not correct because if the adjustment is too tight, the steering wheel will be difficult to turn and if too loose, excessive play in the steering wheel can occur. Answers **b** and **d** are not correct because they do not correctly state the tightening procedure.

25. **The correct answer is d.** A crooked (not straight) steering wheel cannot be caused by a defective upper strut mount, even though it could cause steering problems. Incorrect toe is the major reason for a crooked steering wheel. Answer **a** is not correct because a defective upper strut mount can cause binding. Answer **b** is not correct because a defective upper strut mount could cause noise while the vehicle is being driven over bumps in the road. Answer **c** is not correct because a defective upper strut bearing could have so much friction that the front wheels do not return to the straight ahead position after turning a corner.

26. **The correct answer is d.** Neither technician is correct. The silver/black power steering fluid indicates that aluminum was worn from the control valve area of the rack and pinion steering assembly. The Teflon® sealing rings can wear grooves in the housing. Technician A is not correct because power steering fluid should be amber or red if automatic transmission fluid is used. Technician B is not correct because the gear teeth are not exposed to the power steering fluid in a power rack and pinion steering gear assembly. The rack and pinion gear teeth are lubricated by grease  that is installed during manufacture and is designed to last the life of the vehicle. Answer **c** is not correct because neither technician is correct.

27. **The correct answer is b.** The spring scale is being used to check the force necessary to move the tie rod while it is attached to the inner ball-socket assembly of a rack-and-pinion steering gear. Too little force indicates a worn joint and too much force could indicate a binding joint. Answers **a, c,** and **d** are not correct because they do not indicate the testing of the force needed to move the tie rod for proper ball-socket assembly operation.

28. **The correct answer is c.** The steering damper is used to reduce steering linkage movement, which can result in a steering wheel shimmy while driving over various types of road surfaces. Answer **a** is not correct even though the steering could be difficult to turn if the dampener were to become seized but this is not likely. Answers **b** and **d** are not correct because the dampener does not affect the play in the steering because it is mounted in parallel with the linkage and is not part of the linkage itself.

Suspension and Steering (A4)

B. Suspension Systems Diagnosis and Repair Answers and Explanations

29. **The correct answer is c.** Both technicians are correct. Technician A is correct because noise will be heard from the front suspension if the control arm bushings are worn or deteriorated. The noise may be a squeaking sound or a loud clunking sound if the bushings are partially or completely missing. Technician B is correct because worn or deteriorated strut rod bushings can cause noise when driving over rough roads or during braking or accelerating. Answers **a, b,** and **d** are not correct because both technicians are correct.

30. **The correct answer is b.** Technician B is correct because the weight of the vehicle must be removed (unloaded) from the ball joint to be able to check for excessive free play in the joint itself. Technician A is not correct because if the joint has the weight of the vehicle applied, it is impossible to check for free play in the joint because the weight of the vehicle is being applied to keep the joint together. However, wear indicator-type ball joints must be checked with the weight being applied to the joint, but the question asks how to check for free play and in this case the ball joint has to be unloaded. Answers **c** and **d** are not correct because only Technician B is correct.

31. **The correct answer is c.** Both technicians are correct. Technician A is correct because it is normal for a thin film of oil to be seen at the top of a shock absorber near the seal. If liquid is observed dripping from the shock absorber, then this is a fault and the shock absorber should be replaced. Technician B is correct because cold temperatures can cause the rod seal to bleed a thin layer of fluid and this condition is considered normal. Answers **a, b,** and **d** are not correct because both technicians are correct.

32. **The correct answer is a.** Technician A is correct because the rear left spring center bolt would allow the rear axle to move forward or rearward on one side of the vehicle creating a dog tracking condition. Technician B is not correct because defective upper control arm bushings on the front of the vehicle would not cause the rear of the vehicle to run out of align with the front wheels. Answers **c** and **d** are not correct because only Technician A is correct.

33. **The correct answer is c.** The cotter key *must* be replaced when it is removed because the metal fatigue can cause the end of the cotter key to break off if it is straightened and then bent over a second time. This broken part of the cotter key can become wedged in the wheel bearing, which could cause the wheel to lock leading to a possible collision and personal injury. Answer **a** is not correct because the bearing cup is usually replaced with the bearing and is not replaced as a part of routine service. Answer **b** is not correct even though it should be replaced if the front inner bearings are being serviced. Notice that the question involves servicing just the outer wheel bearings; otherwise, both the seal and the cotter key should be replaced. Answer **d** is not correct because the retainer washer does not wear and its replacement is not necessary.

34. **The correct answer is b.** A defective wheel bearing (brinelled or worn) will cause a hum, rumbling, or growling noise, which increases with vehicle speed similar to the noise of winter tires with an aggressive tread design. Answers **a, c,** and **d** are not correct because these sounds indicate other faults but are not typical of the noise made by a defective wheel bearing.

35. **The correct answer is b.** Technician B is correct because the springs support the weight of the vehicle and if they sag, then replacement springs are needed to restore the proper vehicle height. Technician A is not correct because shock absorbers are designed to dampen the action of the springs and do not support any of the vehicle weight unless special load-lifting-type shock absorbers are installed. Answers **c** and **d** are not correct because only Technician B is correct.

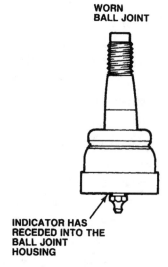

WORN
BALL JOINT

36. **The correct answer is b.** Technician B is correct. The indicator on the ball joint is still visible above the grease fitting. When the ball joint has worn enough to require replacement, the indicator is flush with the base of the joint as shown. Technician A is not correct because the indicator does not show that the ball joint is excessively worn. Answers **c** and **d** are not correct because only Technician B is correct.

INDICATOR HAS
RECEDED INTO THE
BALL JOINT
HOUSING

37. **The correct answer is c.** Both technicians are correct. Technician A is correct because sagging springs would cause the vehicle to ride at a lower than normal height, thereby close to the bump stop. Technician B is also correct because worn shock absorbers can cause the rapid compression of the springs when the vehicle hits a bump in the road causing the suspension to travel farther upward faster than normal. Answers **a, b,** and **d** are not correct because both technicians are correct.

38. **The correct answer is c.** A tie-rod separating tool should be used to separate tapered chassis parts without doing any harm. Answer **a** is not correct because a pickle fork tool often damages the rubber grease seal and should only be used if the joint is to be replaced. Answer **b** is not correct because a torch will not separate a tapered joint and the heat could reduce the strength of the steel parts plus destroying the rubber grease seal. Answer **d** is not correct because a shock or force is required to separate a tapered joint and a drilled hole would ruin the part.

39. **The correct answer is b.** The coil spring *must* be compressed before the strut retaining nut is removed because the spring tension needs to be removed from exerting force on the upper bearing assembly. Failure to compress the spring could result in possible personal injury when the upper retaining nut is removed and the spring expands upward. Answer **a** is not correct because even though the brake caliper and/or brake hose has to be removed on most vehicles in order to remove the strut from the vehicle, it is not necessary to prevent personal injury and may not be needed to be performed on many vehicles. Answers **c** and **d** are not correct because the upper strut mounting bolts and the lower attaching bolt, while often necessary to be removed to replace the strut cartridge, are not necessary to prevent personal injury.

40. **The correct answer is c.** Both technicians are correct. Technician A is correct because an overloaded vehicle can cause the rollers of the bearing to be forced into the outer race (cup) creating dents and causing the bearing to be noisy as the rollers pass over the dents during vehicle travel. Technician B is correct because the rollers could be forced into the outer race causing a dent if the bearings were over tightened, especially if the wheels were not being rotated during the bearing adjustment procedures. Answers **a, b,** and **d** are not correct because both technicians are correct.

41. **The correct answer is a.** Technician A is correct because the weight of the vehicle must be applied to the ball joint to force the indicator into its wear position where it can be observed by the technician. Technician B is not correct because while the free play of the load-carrying ball joints must be checked with the load removed, an indicator-type ball joint is checked with the load of the vehicle on the ball joints. Answers **c** and **d** are not correct because only Technician A is correct.

42. **The correct answer is a.** The drawing shows a large clamp-type tool being used to press a new bushing into the control arm. Answer **b** is not correct because ball joints are not adjustable. Answer **c** is not correct because the drawing shows the control arm bushing area of the control arm rather than the ball joint section, even though a similar operation could be used to replace press-fit-type ball joints. Answer **d** is not correct because control arms are to be replaced rather than straightened if damaged or bent.

46

43. **The correct answer is c.** Both technicians are correct. Technician A is correct because 0.150 in. (150 thousandth of an inch) is greater than the maximum allowable specifications for most vehicles of 0.050 in. (50 thousandth of an inch). Technician B is correct because ball joints should always be replaced as a pair to maintain handling and steering. Answers **a, b,** and **d** are not correct because both technicians are correct.

44. **The correct answer is c.** Defective rear leaf springs can cause the rear of the vehicle to sag thereby causing the left front to rise. Answer **a** is not correct because a broken stabilizer bar link will cause noise from the front and can cause the vehicle to lean excessively when cornering but it is not a load-carrying component so it could not cause the vehicle to sag down in the rear or rise up in the front. Answer **b** is not correct because the track rod keeps the rear wheels tracking properly behind the front wheels and could not cause the described problem. Answer **d** is not correct because a standard shock absorber does not support the vehicle weight and could not cause the problem even though a broken shock absorber could have contributed to the breaking of the rear leaf spring.

45. **The correct answer is b.** A defective strut rod bushing (also called a tension/compression rod bushing) can cause a pull during braking because the lower control arm is able to move toward the rear of the vehicle reducing the caster angle on that side. Answer **a** is not correct because worn or defective stabilizer bar links would cause noise while driving and excessive body lean during cornering, but they would not affect braking because the links do not keep the lower control arm in position. Answer **c** is not correct because even though defective rear leaf springs can cause the vehicle to sag, they are not likely to cause a pull to one side during braking. Answer **d** is not correct because a track rod keeps the rear axle centered under the vehicle and is not likely to cause a pull during braking.

46. **The correct answer is a.** Technician A is correct because a small amount of oil in the strut housing helps transfer heat from the cartridge insert to the outside housing. Without this oil, the strut could overheat causing damage to the seals and valves inside the strut insert. Technician B is not correct because just a small amount of oil is needed to provide a thin film between the cartridge insert and the strut housing. The cartridge insert has its own supply of oil and is a sealed unit. Answers **c** and **d** are not correct because only Technician a is correct.

47. **The correct answer is b.** The rear axle is kept centered under the body by the track rod (panhard rod). If the track rod is bent, the rear axle will be shifted to one side causing it to be out of alignment with the front. Answer **a** is not correct because a rear track bar is not designed to keep the vehicle from swaying when cornering but rather is designed to keep the rear axle centered over the body and acts as one of the major suspension members. Answer **c** is not correct because a track bar would not cause any noise during cornering if bent. Answer **d** is not correct because the track rod is in the rear and would not have a major influence on braking even though it could cause some weird handling.

48. **The correct answer is a.** Technician A is correct because only one of the holes should be totally covered by the coil spring if it has been installed correctly. If the spring was installed upside down, the end of the spring could extend far enough to cover both holes. Technician B is not correct because even though one hole should be covered by the spring, the second hole should be open (not covered) or at least partially covered if the spring has been installed correctly. Answers **c** and **d** are not correct because only Technician A is correct.

49. **The correct answer is c.** Leaking shock absorbers are the least likely cause of vehicle wander when driving on a straight level road. Leaking shock absorbers could cause excessive body movement when traveling over bumps or dips in the road and could cause a harsh ride. Answers **a, b,** and **d** are not correct because all of these components could cause the vehicle to wander due to looseness in the suspension components that allow the front wheels to move left and right as the vehicle is traveling straight.

50. **The correct answer is d.** The least likely cause of a vehicle to sag in the rear would be leaking shock absorbers because even though this condition can cause the vehicle to ride roughly or cause the body to bounce over bumps in the road, the shock absorbers are not a load-carrying component. Answers **a, b,** and **c** are not correct because all of these could cause the rear of the vehicle to sag.

51. **The correct answer is a.** Technician A is correct. If one rear spring is replaced, the other spring on the same axle should also be replaced to maintain the proper ride height and spring rate. Technician B is not correct because, even though replacing shock absorbers would be wise when the springs are installed, they do not contribute to the load-carrying capacity of the suspension system and would not be needed to restore the proper ride height unless special load-carrying shock absorbers are used. The springs support the vehicle weight and the shocks control the action of the springs. Answers **c** and **d** are not correct because Technician A only is correct.

52. **The correct answer is c.** A broken rear control arm or ball joint can cause the top of the left rear wheel to become angled inward at the top because the control arm locates the wheel and allows for up and down movement. Answer **a** is not correct because a worn stabilizer bushing can cause noise during suspension travel and the stabilizer bar is used to control body lean in corners. A fault with a bushing would not cause the wheel to be angled in at the top. Answer **b** is not correct because a broken rear track rod would allow the entire rear suspension to move sideways and would not cause one wheel to be angled inward. Answer **d** is not correct because a shock absorber is not a structural part of the suspension but is rather used to control the movement of the springs.

53. **The correct answer is a.** Worn or defective strut rod bushings will cause a loud clunking sound when the brakes are applied because the strut rods are used to keep the front wheels from moving forward or rearward. When the brakes are applied, the braking force causes the front wheels to move toward the rear. If the bushing is excessively worn or missing, the strut rod contacts the frame creating the loud noise. Answers **b, c,** and **d** are not correct although they would make some noise if defective. They cannot cause a loud clunk when braking.

54. **The correct answer is b.** Technician B is correct because the spring seat insulators isolate the suspension from the body of the vehicle. If one of these spring insulators is damaged or missing, road and suspension noise will be transferred to the body. Technician A is not correct because sagging springs will not cause noise even though the suspension height is not correct. Answers **c** and **d** are not correct because only Technician B is correct.

55. **The correct answer is d.** Sagging springs will cause the vehicle to be lower than normal. If a heavy load has been carried in the vehicle on the left side, the left side springs could have sagged and remained lower than normal even though the load had been removed. Sagging springs require replacement. Answers **a, b,** and **c** are not correct because they do not support the weight of the vehicle and cannot be the cause of the problem.

56. **The correct answer is a.** Technician A is correct because the shock absorbers themselves limit the rear axle travel. If the shocks were removed, the rear axle could drop and cause damage to the brake lines or control arm bushings. Technician B is not correct because the rear springs are attached to the rear axle and while they could fall if the rear axle is lowered, they do not have to be compressed when replacing the rear shock absorbers. Answers **c** and **d** are not correct because only Technician A is correct.

57. **The correct answer is c.** Both technicians are correct. Technician A is correct because all factory and most replacement springs are marked left and right because they are slightly different ratings to compensate for the weight of the driver. Technician B is correct because most springs have to be installed with the correct end facing up to match the spring seats in the frame and on the lower control arm. Answers **a, b,** and **d** are not correct because both technicians are correct.

58. **The correct answer is b.** Technician B only is correct. When the vehicle was hoisted, the suspension is allowed to droop and this is the condition shown. Even though the camber angle looks excessive, the weight of the vehicle will load the suspension and the camber angle will return to normal. Technician A is not correct because the camber angle is not determined with the vehicle off the ground, but rather on a flat level surface with the suspension supporting the full weight of the vehicle. Answers **c** and **d** are not correct because only Technician B is correct.

Suspension and Steering (A4)

C. Wheel Alignment Diagnosis, Adjustment, and Repair
Answers and Explanations

CAMBER

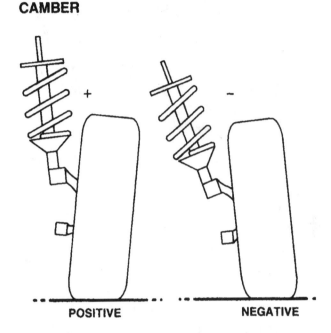

POSITIVE   NEGATIVE

59. **The correct answer is a.** Technician A is correct because camber is a pulling angle if both front wheels are not within 0.5°. Technician B is not correct because while incorrect front toe can cause vehicle handling problems, it is not a pulling angle and therefore, would not cause a pull. Answers **c** and **d** are not correct because only Technician A is correct.

60. **The correct answer is c.** The strut rods adjust caster if they are adjustable. Rotating the adjusting nuts on the strut rod moves the lower control arm forward or rearward thereby moving the lower ball joint and the caster angle. Answers **a** and **b** are not correct because moving the lower ball joint forward or rearward does not change any other angle *directly* except for caster even though camber and toe are somewhat affected by the changes in caster. Answer **d** is not correct because toe-out on turns is determined by the angle of the steering arm and would not change at all if the strut rod is adjusted.

61. **The correct answer is a.** Technician A is correct because a vehicle equipped with an independent front suspension will pull in the direction of the greatest rear toe angle if the rear toe angles are not equal or close to being equal. The rear toe of a vehicle acts like a rudder of a boat and will cause the vehicle to steer in the opposite direction the rear wheels are pointing. Technician B is not correct because incorrect front toe cannot cause pull. Answers **c** and **d** are not correct because only Technician A is correct.

62. **The correct answer is d.** The shims adjust both camber and caster because if shims of equal thickness were removed or added, the camber is changed. If a shim was added or removed from

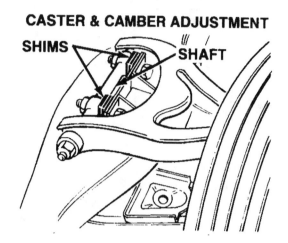

CASTER & CAMBER ADJUSTMENT
SHIMS
SHAFT

either the front or the rear location, then caster and camber would be changed because the upper ball joint would be moved. If a shim is removed from the front and placed in the rear, this caster only is changed while maintaining the same camber. Answers **a** and **b** are not correct because both angles are adjusted. Answer **c** is not correct because even though the toe angle will change, it is not directly changed by adding or removing shims.

63. **The correct answer is c.** Both technicians are correct. Technician A is correct because the extra weight of the camper will cause the springs to compress, which usually changes the camber and caster. Technician B is correct because the extra weight of the camper will cause the front toe angle to change as the camber changes when the springs compress. The truck should be aligned with the camper installed to avoid handling or tire wear problems. Answers **a, b,** and **d** are not correct because both technicians are correct.

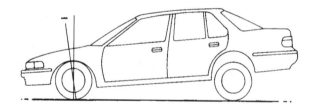

64. **The correct answer is a.** The vehicle will pull to the right because the right front camber is greater than the left front camber by 0.7 degree. Both front tires will feather edge because the toe is not within specifications. Answer **b** is not correct because the vehicle will pull to the side with the most camber (right). Answer **c** is not correct because the tire wear will occur on the inside edges of both front tires due to the excessive toe-out. Answer **d** is not correct because even though the vehicle will wear the inside of both front tires, it will pull to the right, not to the left.

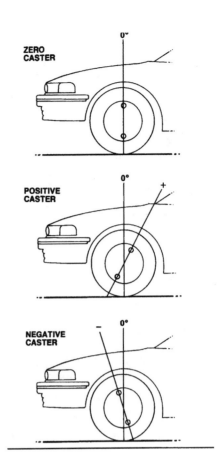

65. **The correct answer is b.** The vehicle will pull toward the right because the caster is unequal by 1.8° and will pull toward the side with the least amount of caster. Answer **a** is not correct because the difference in the caster angle will cause the vehicle to pull toward the right. Answer **c** is not correct because the vehicle will pull rather than be unstable, which would cause wandering. Answer **d** is not correct because the vehicle will pull toward the right due to the caster difference rather than to the left.

66. **The correct answer is c.** The alignment will cause the vehicle to pull toward the right due to the difference in the caster angles (pulls toward the side with the least caster). Answer **a** (wander) is not correct because a vehicle cannot wander if it is pulling to one side. Wander is usually caused by a toe out condition and this vehicle has the specified (within range) toe in. Answer **b** is not correct because the two tire wearing angles, camber and toe, are within factory specified limits and therefore excessive tire wear should not be a concern. The vehicle will pull due to the difference in the front caster angles. Answer **d** is not correct because the vehicle will pull to the right, not the left, and will not feather-edge the tires because front toe is within factory specifications.

67. **The correct answer is a.** Technician A is correct because the tire wear and pulling are consistent with the symptoms that would be created if the camber on the right front was excessively positive. This situation could occur if the vehicle had struck a curb and had bent the lower control arm. Technician B is not correct because incorrectly adjusted caster angles will not cause tire wear on one edge only. Answers **c** and **d** are not correct because only Technician A is correct.

68. **The correct answer is a.** Toe is the alignment angle that most often requires adjustment and will wear the tires if not within factory specifications. Answer **b** is not correct because even though incorrect camber can cause tire wear, it is not as important as toe and is less often in need of adjustment. Answer **c** is not correct because caster does not directly affect tire wear especially compared to incorrect toe setting. Answer **d** is not correct because SAI (steering axis inclination) is not an adjustable angle in most cases and has little affect on tire wear even though it can affect vehicle handling if it is not within factory specifications.

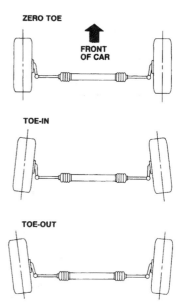

69. **The correct answer is c.** Torque steer occurs when engine torque is applied unequally to the front drive wheels thereby creating a pull that is noticeable during rapid acceleration. Answers **a, b**, and **d** are not correct because even though these components can cause a pull, they are not likely to cause a pull only during acceleration.

70. **The correct answer is a.** Technician A is correct because a vehicle will pull to the side with the most camber (highest positive camber or the lowest negative camber angles). Technician B is not correct because even if there is unequal toe between the left and right side, the toe angle splits when the vehicle is being driven and the steering wheel is forced crooked as the front wheels align themselves. Answers **c** and **d** are not correct because only Technician A is correct.

71. **The correct answer is a.** Technician A is correct because this condition (often called memory steer) occurs when there is a binding in the steering that creates a force to be applied to the steering linkage and results in a pull that can change from one direction to the other. Technician B is not correct because excessive positive caster creates a force on the suspension that tends to force the steering wheel to a straight ahead position rather than to one direction or the other. Answers **c** and **d** are not correct because only Technician A is correct.

72. **The correct answer is d.** Neither technician is correct. Technician A is not correct because the alignment angles are not changed when tires/wheels are installed even though the wheel offset difference could cause some handling concerns for the driver. Technician B is not correct because the suspension angles are not changed when different size wheels and tires are installed even though the handling may be changed as a result. Answers **a, b,** and **c** are not correct because neither technician is correct.

73. **The correct answer is d.** The angle of the steering knuckle (arm) determines the amount of toe-out-on- turns (TOOT), also called the Ackerman effect, and therefore, if this measurement is not within factory specifications, the steering arm is likely damaged in a collision. Answers **a, b,** and **c** are not correct because these items do not affect the toe-out-on-turn angles(s).

ACKERMANN EFFECT

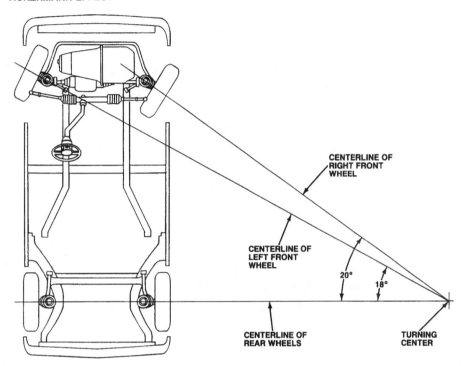

74. **The correct answer is c.** The rear toe angle determines the thrust angle. The rear toe is similar to a rudder on a boat and affects the direction of vehicle travel. Answer **a** is not correct because the thrust angle is the total of both rear wheels, not the camber angle. Answer **b** is not correct because the front angles do not affect the rear thrust angle. Answer **d** is not correct because rear caster is not measured or adjustable on the rear and would not affect the rear thrust angle.

75. **The correct answer is c.** The rear toe should be the first angle adjusted if needed because the front wheels (toe) are then set parallel to the rear to achieve the proper vehicle tracking. Answers **a, b,** and **d** are not correct because even though the angles should be adjusted if out of factory specification, they are not the first angle that should be adjusted.

76. **The correct answer is a.** The wedge will move the axle hub outward at the top, thereby increasing camber. Answer **b** is not correct because the wedge is being installed vertically and would move the top of the wheel outward. To change toe, the wedge would have to be installed toward the front or rear of the vehicle. Answer **c** is not correct because rear caster is not changeable and if it were, the pivot point of the lower control arm would need to be moved forward or rearward. Answer **d** is not correct because rear SAI is not measured or corrected.

77. **The correct answer is d.** Neither technician is correct. Technician A is not correct because front camber and toe are within specifications. It would require negative camber or a toe out condition to cause tire wear on the inside edges of the front tires. Technician B is not correct because the rear toe is within specifications. Answers **a, b,** and **c** are not correct because neither technician is correct.

78. **The correct answer is b.** Technician B is correct because zero is an acceptable reading for toe, which indicates that both front wheels are traveling straight. Technician A is not correct because the total rear toe is within factory specifications and will not cause a dog tracking condition. Answers **c** and **d** are not correct because only Technician B is correct.

79. **The correct answer is c.** The present alignment is not perfect but the vehicle would most likely track left. The caster difference (0.7°) would indicate a slight tendency to pull to the left and the camber difference (0.6°) also would cause a pull to the left. Answers **a** and **b** are not correct because the vehicle will pull to the left. Answer **d** is not correct because a wander is usually caused by a lack of directional control and in this situation the vehicle will pull to the left.

80. **The correct answer is c.** Both technicians are correct. Technician A is correct because low tire pressures can cause the vehicle to wander due to the lack of sidewall support of the tires. Technician B is correct because loose steering linkage can cause the vehicle to travel first one direction, then the other, causing the vehicle to wander. Answers **a, b,** and **d** are not correct because both technicians are correct.

81. **The correct answer is c.** To straighten the steering wheel, the technician should adjust the toe by rotating the tie rod sleeves or adjusters with the steering wheel in the straight ahead position. Answer **a** is not correct because this method would not allow the steering gear to be centered, thereby creating a concern especially if the vehicle is equipped with a variable ratio steering gear. Answer **b** is not correct because adjusting the camber will not straighten the steering wheel. Answer **d** is not correct because adjusting the caster angle will not straighten the steering wheel.

82. **The correct answer is d.** A bent strut is the most likely cause because the SAI is the angle of the upper strut mount and the lower pivot (ball joint). The camber is under specifications, as well as the included angle (camber plus SAI), which indicates that there is a bent strut. Answer **a** is not correct because the camber and included angle should be close to equal and within factory specifications. Answers **b** and **c** are not correct because worn ball joints or tie rod ends will not cause the camber and the included angle to be out of specifications.

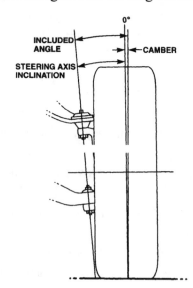

83. **The correct answer is b.** The angle of the steering arms determines the Ackerman angle (toe out on turns) or the amount that the wheels rotate when turning. The inside wheel turns at a greater angle than the outside wheel to allow for the greater distance the outside wheel must travel. If the steering arm (steering knuckle) is bent, the front wheel(s) will not turn to the proper angle and the tire(s) will squeal due to the slipping of the tread across the pavement. Answers **a, c,** and **d** are not correct because even though this can cause steering-related problems, they are not the most likely to cause this particular problem of slow speed tire squeal.

84. **The correct answer is a.** Technician A is correct because if the engine cradle was shifted to the left, the lower control for the left side would be moved toward the outside, which would decrease the camber reading on the left and increase the camber reading on the right. Technician B is not correct because even though a leaking strut could cause a handling problem, it cannot cause the camber angle to decrease on the left and increase on the right. Answers **c** and **d** are not correct because only Technician A is correct.

85. **The correct answer is b.** Technician B is correct because the difference in the rear toe will cause the vehicle to pull toward the side that has the greatest amount of toe just as a rudder is used to steer a boat. Technician A is not correct because unlike the rear wheels, the front wheels are tied together with tie rods and this causes the toe to split equally as the vehicle is driven. Answers **c** and **d** are not correct because only Technician B is correct.

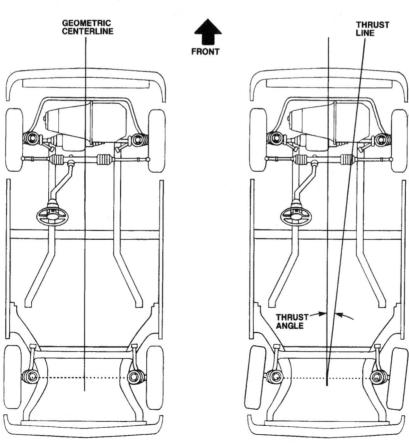

86. **The correct answer is d.** Neither technician is correct. Technician A is not correct because incorrect camber cannot cause a tramp-type vibration even though it can cause excessive tire wear and/or a pulling condition if not corrected. Technician B is not correct because incorrect toe can cause excessive tire wear and an off center steering wheel, but it cannot cause a tramp-type vibration. Only a fault with a wheel or tire can cause a tramp-type vibration. Answer **c** is not correct because neither technician is correct.

87. **The correct answer is c.** The cam bolts are able to change camber if both are rotated the same direction by the same amount. Caster is adjusted by rotating one cam only or both in opposite directions to maintain the same camber. Answers **a, b,** and **d** are not correct because camber and caster can be adjusted.

88. **The correct answer is b.** The shim is positioned so that the camber will be changed (outward at the bottom to decrease camber). Answer **a** is not correct because to change toe and camber, the shim would need to be placed toward the front or rear of the hub. Answer **c** is not correct because the shim would need to be placed at the front or rear of the hub to change the toe, not at the bottom as shown. Answer **d** is not correct because caster cannot be changed using a shim and is not adjusted on the rear of a vehicle.

89. **The correct answer is c.** The camber will be adjusted by rotating the eccentric cam at the base of the strut. Answer **a** is not correct because caster will not be changed. Answer **b** is not correct because even though the toe will change slightly when the eccentric is rotated, the toe change is due to the change in the camber. Answer **d** is not correct because neither the SAI nor the caster is changed when the eccentric is rotated.

90. **The correct answer is b.** When shims are added to both the front and rear positions, the control arm will be moved toward the right, thereby increasing positive camber. Answer **a** is not correct because adding shims to the front position will increase camber but it will also increase caster by moving the ball joint rearward. Answer **c** is not correct because moving shim(s) from the front to the rear will decrease caster and keep the camber about the same. Answer **d** is not correct because removing shims will decrease camber, not increase camber.

91. **The correct answer is b.** By adjusting the strut rod, the lower control arm is moved forward or rearward, thereby changing the caster angle. Answer **a** is not correct because even though the camber angle may change as the strut rod is adjusted, it is the result of the change in the caster angle that caused the change in the camber. Answer **c** is not correct because even though the toe will change, it is a result of the change in the caster angle. Answer **d** is not correct because toe-out-on-turns is not adjustable but rather is built into the angle of the steering arms.

Suspension and Steering (A4)

D. Wheel and Tire Diagnosis and Repair Answers and Explanations

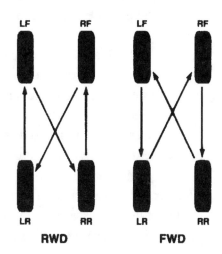

92. **The correct answer is c.** Using the modified X tire rotation method, the driven wheels are moved straight forward or rearward and the non-drive wheels are crossed as they are moved forward or rearward. In a front-wheel drive vehicle, the front wheels are moved straight back so the right front would be placed on the right rear. Answers **a, b,** and **d** are not correct because they do not place the wheel in the correct position using the modified X tire rotation method.

93. **The correct answer is a.** Most vehicle manufacturers specify a wheel tightening torque of about 80 to 100 lb-ft and even though some may be less than 80 lb-ft or greater than 100 lb-ft, this is the best answer. Answers **b, c,** and **d** are not correct because they are higher than the usual specified wheel lug nut torque for passenger vehicles.

94. **The correct answer is b.** Under inflated tires will cause the tires to wear excessively on both the inside and outside edges. Answer **a** is not correct because over inflation rather than under inflation will cause excessive tire wear in the center of the tread. Answer **c** is not correct because excessive radial runout will cause a tramp-type vibration, but is unlikely to cause tire wear on both edges. Answer **d** is not correct because excessive lateral runout will cause a shimmy-type vibration, but is unlikely to cause tire wear on both edges.

95. **The correct answer is b.** Never exceed 40 psi when seating the bead of the tire during installation, as a rim or bead damage can occur, which could cause personal injury. After the tire bead has been seated, the specified amount of air pressure can be used. Answers **a, c,** and **d** are not correct because they do not state the industry standard for maximum pressure during tire installation.

96. **The correct answer is b.** Coated or painted lead wheel weights should be used to help prevent corrosion damage to an alloy or aluminum wheel, which can occur due to moisture and the use of two different metals in contact. Answers **a, c,** and **d** are not correct because these are not the recommended type of weights to use on alloy or aluminum wheels.

58

97. **The correct answer is c.** Both technicians are correct. Technician A is correct because the lug nuts should be tightened in a star pattern to insure that the wheels are installed with even clamping force. Technician B is correct because a torque wrench should be used to not only be assured that the proper torque is applied to the lug nut, but to ensure that all of the nuts are tightened to the same torque to help avoid wheel or brake rotor distortion. Answers **a, b,** and **d** are not correct because both technicians are correct.

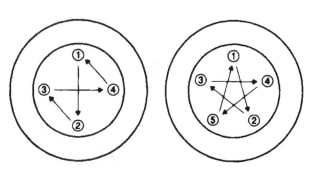

FOUR-NUT WHEEL   **FIVE-NUT WHEEL**

98. **The correct answer is a.** Technician A is correct because when match mounting, the highest portion of the tire (usually at or near the major splice) is aligned with the valve core, which is usually drilled at the smallest diameter of the wheel, resulting in a smoother ride and less weight needed to balance the tire/wheel assembly. Technician B is not correct because only a material that is approved for tire mounting should be used. The use of silicone spray lubricant could cause the tire to rotate on the rim during braking. Answers **c** and **d** are not correct because only Technician A is correct.

99. **The correct answer is a.** Technician A is correct because all tires and wheels are not perfectly round and some minor differences may have caused the excessive radial runout (out of round). By rotating the tire on the rim, the high spot of the tire may be aligned with the low spot of the wheel, which could reduce the total amount of runout. Technician B is not correct because even though the tires could be defective and require replacement, the tires should be rotated on the rim and then checked again for excessive runout before replacement. Answers **c** and **d** are not correct because only Technician A is correct.

100. **The correct answer is c.** Both technicians are correct. Technician A is correct because if the wheel is bent, the lateral runout could be excessive. The excessive lateral runout could occur if the vehicle hit or slid into a curb. Technician B is correct because the mounting hub could have excessive lateral runout, which would be transferred and the amount amplified at the outer diameter of the wheel. Hub or spindle replacement may be necessary to correct the excessive runout. Answers **c** and **d** are not correct because both technicians are correct.

101. **The correct answer is a.** Diagonal tire wear is shown and is a result of incorrect toe setting on the rear of a front-wheel-drive vehicle. The wear pattern is created by the tire being dragged sideways as it rotates. Answer **b** is not correct because incorrect camber will cause excessive tire wear on one side of the tread. Answer **c** is not correct because an over inflated tire will be worn more in the center of the tread compared to the outside edges. Answer **d** is not correct because an under inflated tire will cause excessive wear on both the inside and outside edges of the tread.

102. **The correct answer is c.** An air impact wrench not only exerts more than the specified lug nut torque, but also cannot be controlled to provide an equal amount of torque to all nuts, which results in a possible warpage condition. Answer **a** is not correct because even though the lug nuts may be more difficult to remove if an air impact wrench is used, the primary reason for using a torque wrench or torque absorbing adapters is to prevent doing harm to the vehicle. The best answer is **c**. Answer **b** is not correct because harm can occur including permanent warpage of the wheel and/or disc brake rotor. Answer **d** is not correct because even though warpage can occur that causes a vibration, the use of an air impact wrench cannot cause a tramp-type vibration or out of balance condition.

103. **The correct answer is b.** Technician B is correct because an imbalance in the front wheels or tires is often felt in the steering wheel. Technician A is not correct because an out of balance drive shaft will often cause a vibration in the seat rather than just in the steering wheel. Answers **c** and **d** are not correct because only Technician B is correct.

Suspension and Steering (A4)

Appendix 1 – Environmental Questions

All automotive service operations assume that the service technician will adhere to proper handling and disposal of all automotive waste. Questions about environmental issues are not asked on the actual ASE test, but these sample questions will test your knowledge of the proper ways to handle these issues.

1.   Hazardous materials include all of the following except _____.

        a.   Engine oil
        b.   Asbestos
        c.   Water
        d.   Brake cleaner

2.   To determine if a product or substance being used is hazardous, consult _____.

        a.   A dictionary
        b.   A MSDS
        c.   SAE standards
        d.   EPA guidelines

3.   Technician A says that used engine oil can be used in waste oil heaters. Technician B says that waste oil can be recycled by a licensed recycler. Which technician is correct?

        a.   Technician A only
        b.   Technician B only
        c.   Both Technicians A and B
        d.   Neither Technician A nor B

4.   Two technicians are discussing what to do with used antifreeze coolant. Technician A says that it can be recycled either onsite or offsite. Technician B says that it can be poured down the drain. Which technician is correct?

        a.   Technician A only
        b.   Technician B only
        c.   Both Technicians A and B
        d.   Neither Technician A nor B

5.   Used antifreeze coolant is often considered hazardous waste because it contains _____.

        a.   Ethyl glycol
        b.   Water (H_2O)
        c.   Dissolved metal(s)
        d.   Organic acids

6. Two technicians are discussing corrosive materials. Technician A says that a substance with a pH of 2 or lower is a strong acid. Technician B says that a substance with a pH of 12.5 or higher is caustic. Which technician is correct?

    a. Technician A only
    b. Technician B only
    c. Both Technicians A and B
    d. Neither Technician A nor B

7. Two technicians are discussing material safety data sheets (MSDS). Technician A says to look for the ingredients that contain the letters "clor" or "fluor". Technician B says to look for a flash point below 140°F (60°C). Which technician is correct?

    a. Technician A only
    b. Technician B only
    c. Both Technicians A and B
    d. Neither Technician A nor B

8. Two technicians are discussing used batteries. Technician A says that they should be considered hazardous waste and should be recycled by a licensed recycler. Technician B says to store used batteries near a drain in case they leak acid. Which technician is correct?

    a. Technician A only
    b. Technician B only
    c. Both Technicians A and B
    d. Neither Technician A nor B

9. Technician A says that gasoline should always be stored in red containers. Technician B says that gasoline should always be stored in sealed containers. Which technician is correct?

    a. Technician A only
    b. Technician B only
    c. Both Technicians A and B
    d. Neither Technician A nor B

10. Hazardous waste should be handled by the shop or repair facility and records kept of which of the following:

    a. Name of the company or individual that disposes of the waste
    b. Where it is being sent
    c. What is going to happen to the waste
    d. All of the above

Suspension and Steering (A4)

Appendix 1 – Environmental Answers

1. **The correct answer is c.** Water is not considered to be a hazardous material unless it is contaminated by other elements that are considered to be hazardous. Answer **c** is not correct because engine oil is considered to be hazardous because of the dissolved metals and accumulated acid that used oil contains. Answer **b** is not correct because asbestos is considered to be a cancer causing material if breathed. Answer **d** is not correct because brake cleaner often contains solvents or other volatile organic compounds (VOL) that are considered to be hazardous.

2. **The correct answer is b.** The material safety data sheet (MSDS) is the best source for information regarding a product or substance. Answer **a** is not correct because a product or substance is often a combination of ingredients and would not be listed or described in a dictionary. Answers **c** and **d** are not correct because even though these organizations have established standards, the product or substance could meet these standards and still be considered hazardous.

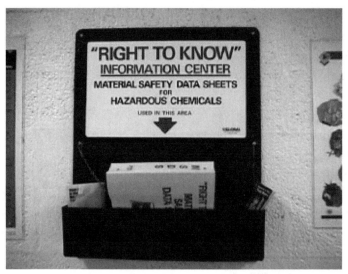

3. **The correct answer is c.** Technician A is correct because waste oil can be burned in a waste oil heater with a capacity of less than 500,000 BTUs. Technician B is correct because used (waste) oil can be recycled by a licensed recycler. Answers **a**, **b**, and **d** are not correct because both technicians are correct.

4. **The correct answer is a.** Used antifreeze coolant can be recycled either on site or shipped to a licensed recycler off site. Technician B is not correct because unless a permit is applied for and granted, it is generally not acceptable to pour used coolant down a sanitary sewer. Answers **c** and **d** are not correct because only Technician A is correct.

5. **The correct answer is c.** Antifreeze coolant (ethylene glycol) by itself is not considered to be hazardous. When the coolant is used in an engine, it can absorb metals such as iron, steel, copper, and lead from the cooling system components, which can cause the coolant to become hazardous. Answer **a** is not correct because most coolant is mostly ethylene glycol with about 5% additives and by itself is not considered to be hazardous. Answer **b** is not correct because even though water containing chemicals can be considered to be hazardous, water by itself is not hazardous. Answer **d** is not correct because the acid content would have to be high enough to lower the pH form about 7-12 down to 2 or less to be considered hazardous.

6. **The correct answer is c.** Technician A is correct because a pH of 2 or less is considered to be strong acid and is very corrosive. Technician B is correct because any substance with a pH of 12.5 or higher is very caustic and is considered to be hazardous. Answers **a**, **b**, and **d** are not correct because both technicians are correct.

7. **The correct answer is c.** Technician A is correct because most hazardous materials contain chemicals that have the letter "clor" or "fluor" in their ingredients as described in the material safety data sheet (MSDS). Technician B is correct because a material is considered to be hazardous if it has a flash point (temperature where it will ignite) below 140°F (60°C). Gasoline is an example of a product that has a flash temperature below 140°F. Answers **a**, **b**, and **d** are not correct because both technicians are correct.

8. **The correct answer is a.** Used batteries should be recycled and transported to an EPA approved recycling facility. Answer **b** is not correct because batteries should be stored away from drains to prevent the possibility that battery acid could seep into the sanitary or storm sewer. Answers **c** and **d** are not correct because only Technician A is correct.

9. **The correct answer is c.** Technician A is correct because gasoline should only be stored in red containers for easy identification. Technician B is correct because gasoline should always be stored in a sealed container to prevent the escape of gasoline fumes, which could be easily ignited. Answers **a**, **b**, and **d** are not correct because both technicians are correct.

10. **The correct answer is d.** A shop handling hazardous waste must keep records which include **a** the name of the company or individual that disposes of the waste, **b** the location where the material is sent, and **c** how the waste is going to be disposed of when it reaches the site. Answers **a**, **b**, and **c** are not correct because all three answers are correct.

Suspension and Steering (A4)

Appendix 2 – Safety Questions

All automotive service operations assume that the service technician will practice safe work habits. Questions about safety issues are not asked on the actual ASE test, but these sample questions will test your knowledge of the proper ways to handle these issues.

1. All equipment used in the shop must be designed to meet what safety standards?

    a. Occupational Safety and Health Act (OSHA)
    b. Environmental Protection Agency (EPA)
    c. Resource Conservation and Recovery Act (RCRA)
    d. Workplace Hazardous Material Information Systems (WHMIS)

2. All items are considered to be personal protection equipment (PPE) **except**:

    a. Safety glasses
    b. Gloves
    c. Hearing protection
    d. Hair net

3. When should service technicians wear ear protection?

    a. If the sound level is high enough that you must raise your voice to be heard
    b. Above 90 dB (a lawnmower is about 110 dB)
    c. When using a torch
    d. Both a and b

4. A service technician should _____.

    a. Pull on a wrench
    b. Push on a wrench
    c. Use your legs when lifting heavy loads
    d. Both a and c

5. A three-prong 110-volt plug is being used, but it will not fit the two-prong outlet. What should the technician do?

    a. Cut off the round ground prong
    b. Use an adapter from the three-prong plug to the two-prong electrical outlet
    c. Attach a grounded adapter and connect the green ground wire to the outlet housing before using the electrical device
    d. Use a cordless tool

6. Personal protection equipment (PPE) can include _____.

    a. Steel-toe shoes
    b. Face mask
    c. Gloves
    d. All of the above

7. The shop should have _____.

    a. Guards in good condition installed on machinery
    b. Shop/bay floors that are clean and dry
    c. Fire extinguishers that are properly charged and easily accessible
    d. All of the above

8. What type of fire extinguisher should be used to put out an oil or grease fire?

    a. Water
    b. CO_2
    c. Dry chemical
    d. Either b or c

9. To what does the term "lockout" or LO/TO refer?

    a. A union strike
    b. A lock placed on the lever that disconnects electrical power
    c. A type of hand tool
    d. A safety ground fault switch

10. A service technician should wear personal protection equipment to be protected against all **except** _____.

    a. Used oil
    b. Pumice-type cleaners
    c. Falling heavy objects
    d. Loud noises

Suspension and Steering (A4)

Appendix 2 – Safety Question Answers

1. **The correct answer is a.** Shop equipment must meet the standards established by the Occupational Safety and Health Act (OSHA). Answers **b**, **c**, and **d** are not correct because the EPA, RCRA, and WHMIS regulate air, water, ground contamination, and hazardous materials and are not associated with the specifications of shop equipment.

2. **The correct answer is d.** Answer **d** is correct; a hair net is used to prevent hair from falling into food and is not generally considered to be safety equipment, even though long hair could get caught in machinery. Answers **a**, **b**, and **c** are all considered to be personal protection equipment.

3. **The correct answer is d.** Answer **a** is correct because ear protection should be worn if the surrounding noise level is high enough that it requires you to raise your voice to be heard. Answer **b** is correct because the OSHA standard requires that ear protection be used whenever noise levels exceed 90 dB. Answer **c** is not correct because a torch will usually not create noise above 90 dB.

4. **The correct answer is d.** Answer **a** is correct because a technician should pull (instead of push) a wrench. Answer **c** is correct because a technician should use his/her legs and not his/her back to lift heavy objects. Answer **b** is not correct because a technician could be injured by pushing on a wrench when the fastener breaks loose or if the wrench slips.

5. **The correct answer is c.** Answer **c** is correct because a three-prong plug to a two-prong electrical outlet adapter has a green wire pigtail that should be attached to the outlet box to be assured that the device is properly grounded. Answer **a** is not correct because if the ground prong is cut off, the device has no electrical path to ground and could create a shock hazard. Answer **b** is not correct because simply using an adapter without grounding the adapter prevents the device from being properly grounded, which could cause a shock hazard. Answer **d** is not correct because even though a cordless tool would not create a hazard, the question states that a three-prong plug is being used and the best answer is **c**.

6. **The correct answer is d.** Answers **a**, **b**, and **c** are correct because steel-toe shoes, face mask, and gloves are all considered to be personal protection equipment (PPE). Answers **a**, **b**, and **c** are not correct because all three items are considered to be PPE, not just one of the items.

7. **The correct answer is d.** Answer **a** is correct because guards must be installed on all machinery that requires a guard and they must be in good condition. Answer **b** is correct because the shop/bay floors should be clean and dry to prevent slippage, which could cause personal injury. Answer **c** is correct because fire extinguishers must be fully charged and easily accessible. Answers **a**, **b**, and **c** are not correct because all three items should be present in all shops.

8. **The correct answer is d.** Answer **b** is correct because a CO_2 fire extinguisher can be used on almost any type of fire including an oil or grease fire. Answer **c** is correct because a dry chemical fire extinguisher can also be used on most types of fires including an oil and grease fire. Answer **a** is not correct because water is heavier than oil and will cause the oil to float on the surface of the water.

9. **The correct answer is b.** Answer **b** is correct because the term lock out/try out (LO/TO) refers to physically installing a lock on the electrical box that would prevent the accidental switching on of electrical power to the circuit being serviced. Answer **a** is not correct because even though the term lockout is used to describe some actions, the term LO/TO is used mostly to describe the locking out of an electrical circuit. Answers **c** and **d** are not correct because they do not describe the locking out of electrical power.

10. **The correct answer is b.** Answer **b** is correct because pumice-type cleaners are typically used to wash hands and are not considered to be hazardous. Answers **a**, **c**, and **d** are not correct because the question asks which is not a possible hazardous material.

A4 English-Language Glossary

Ackerman principle - The angle of the steering arms causes the inside wheel to turn more sharply than the outer wheel when making a turn. This produces toe-out on turns (TOOT).

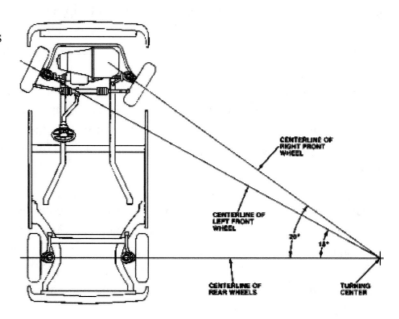

Alemite fitting - *See* Zerk.

Anti-dive - A term used to describe the geometry of the suspension that controls the movement of the vehicle during braking. It is normal for a vehicle to nose-dive slightly during braking and is designed into most vehicles.

Anti-roll bar - *See* stabilizer bar.

Anti-squat - A term used to describe the geometry of the suspension that controls the movement of the vehicle body during acceleration. 100% anti-squat means that the body remains level during acceleration. Less than 100% indicates that the body "squats down," or lowers in the rear during acceleration.

Anti-sway bar - *See* Stabilizer bar.

Articulation test - A test specified by some vehicle manufacturers that tests the amount of force necessary to move the inner tie rod end in the ball socket assembly. The usual specification for this test is greater than 1lb (4 N) and less than 6 lb (26 N) of force.

ASE - Abbreviation for the National Institute for Automotive Service Excellence, a nonprofit organization for the testing and certification of vehicle service technicians.

Aspect ratio - The ratio of height to width of a tire. A tire with an aspect ratio of 60 (a 60 series tire) has a height (from rim to tread) of 60% of its cross-sectional width.

Axial - In line along with the axis or centerline of a part or component. Axial play in a ball joint means looseness in the same axis as the ball joint stud.

Back spacing - The distance between the back rim edge and the center section mounting pad of a wheel.

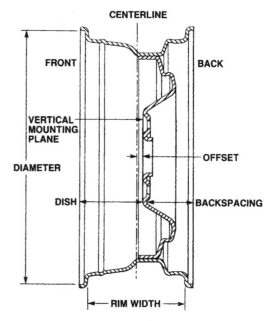

Backside setting - *See* Back spacing.

Ball socket assembly - An inner tie rod end assembly that contains a ball and socket joint at the point where the assembly is threaded on to the end of the steering rack.

Bolt circle - The diameter (in inches or millimeters) of a circle drawn through the center of the bolt holes in a wheel.

Bounce test - A test used to check the condition of shock absorbers.

Breather tube - A tube that connects the left and right bellows of a rack and pinion steering gear.

Brinelling - A type of mechanical failure used to describe a dent in metal such as that which occurs when a shock load is applied to a bearing. Named after Johann A. Brinell, a Swedish engineer.

Bump steer - Used to describe what occurs when the steering linkage is not level, causing the front tires to turn inward or outward as the wheels and suspension move up and down. Automotive chassis engineers call it *roll steer.*

Bump stop - *See* Jounce bumper.

CAMBER

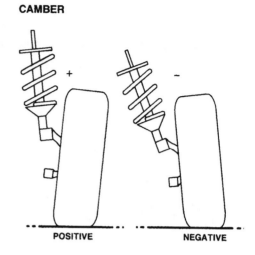

Camber - The inward or outward tilt of the wheels from true vertical as viewed from the front or rear of the vehicle. Positive camber means the top of the wheel is out from center of the vehicle more than the bottom of the wheel.

Cardan joint - A type of universal joint named for a sixteenth-century Italian mathematician.

Caster - The forward or backward tilt of an imaginary line drawn through the steering axis as viewed from the side of the vehicle. Positive caster is where an imaginary line would contact the road surface in front of the contact path of the tire.

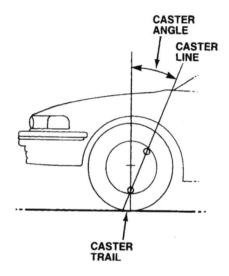

Caster sweep - A process used to measure caster during a wheel alignment procedure where the front wheels are rotated first inward, then outward, a specified amount.

Center bolt - A bolt used to hold the leaves of a leaf spring together in the center. Also called a *centering pin.*

Center support bearing - A bearing used to support the center of a long drive shaft on a rear-wheel-drive vehicle. Also called a *steady bearing.*

Centering pin - *See* Center bolt.

Centerline steering - Used to describe the position of the steering wheel while driving on a straight, level road. The steering wheel should be centered or within plus or minus 3°, as specified by many vehicle manufacturers.

Chassis - The frame, suspension, steering and machinery of a motor vehicle.

Coefficient of friction - A measure of the amount of friction, usually measured from 0 to 1. A low number (0.3) indicates low friction, and a high number (0.9) indicates high friction.

Coil spring - A spring steel rod wound in a spiral (helix) shape. Used in both front and rear suspension systems.

Compensation - A process used during a wheel alignment procedure where the sensors are calibrated to eliminate errors in the alignment readings that may be the result of a bent wheel or unequal installation of the sensor on the wheel of the vehicle.

Composite - A term used to describe the combining of individual parts into a larger component. For example, a composite leaf spring is constructed of fiberglass and epoxy; a composite master brake cylinder contains both plastic parts (reservoir) and metal parts (cylinder housing).

Compression bumper - *See* Jounce bumper.

Compression rod - *See* Strut rod.

Cone - The inner race or ring of a bearing.

Constant velocity joint - Commonly called *CV joints*. CV joints are drive line joints that can transmit engine power through relatively large angles without a change in the velocity, as is usually the case with conventional Cardan-type U-joints.

Cotter key - A metal loop used to retain castle nuts by being installed through a hole. Size is measured by diameter and length (for example, 1/8" x 1 1/2"). Also called a *cotter pin*. Named for the old English verb meaning "to close or fasten."

Coupling disc - *See* Flexible coupling.

Cow catcher - A large spring seat used on many General Motors MacPherson strut units. If the coil spring breaks, the cow catcher prevents one end of the spring from moving outward and cutting a tire.

Cross camber/caster - The difference of angle from one side of the vehicle to the other. Most manufacturers recommend a maximum difference side to side of 1/2° for camber and caster.

Cross steer - A type of steering linkage commonly used on light and medium trucks.

Cup - The outer race or ring of a bearing.

CV joints - Constant velocity joints.

Differential - A mechanical unit containing gears that provides gear reduction and a change of direction of engine power and permits the drive wheels to rotate at different speeds, as required when turning a corner.

Directional stability - Ability of a vehicle to move forward in a straight line with a minimum of driver control. Crosswinds and road irregularities will have little effect if directional stability is good.

Dog tracking - The condition where the rear wheels do not follow directly behind the front wheels. Named for dogs that run with their rear paws offset toward one side so that their rear paws will not hit their front paws.

DOT - The Department of Transportation.

Double Cardan - A universal joint that uses two conventional Cardan joints together, to allow the joint to operate at greater angles.
Drag link - Used to describe a link in the center of the steering linkage; usually called a *center link*.

Drag rod - *See* Strut rod.

Drift - A mild pull that does not cause a force on the steering wheel that the driver must counteract (also known as lead). Also refers to a tapered tool used to center a component in a bolt hole prior to installing the bolt.

Dropping point - The temperature at which a grease passes from a semisolid to a liquid state under conditions specified by ASTM.

Dry park test - A test of steering and/or suspension components. With the wheels in the straight-ahead position and the vehicle on flat level ground, have an assistant turn the steering wheel while you are looking and touching all steering and suspension components, checking for any looseness.

Durometer - The hardness rating of rubber products, named for an instrument used to measure hardness that was developed about 1890.

Dust cap - A functional metal cap that keeps grease in and dirt out of wheel bearings. Also called a *grease cap*.

Flexible coupling - A part of the steering mechanism between the steering column and the steering gear or rack and pinion assembly. Also called a *rag joint* or *steering coupling disc*. The purpose of the flexible coupling is to keep noise vibration and harshness from being transmitted from the road and steering to the steering wheel.

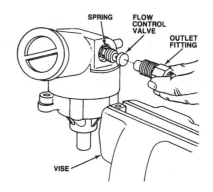

Flow control valve - Regulates and controls the flow of power steering pump hydraulic fluids to the steering gear or rack and pinion assembly. The flow control valve is usually part of the power steering pump assembly.

Follower ball joint - A ball joint used in a suspension system to provide support and control without having the weight of the vehicle or the action of the springs transferred through the joint itself. Also called a *friction ball joint.*

Forward steer - *See* Front steer.

4 x 4 - The term used to describe a four-wheel-drive vehicle. The first "4" indicates the number of wheels of the vehicle; the second "4" indicates the number of wheels that are driven by the engine.

4 x 2 - The term used to describe a two-wheel-drive truck. The "4" indicates the number of wheels of the vehicle; the "2" indicates the number of wheels that are driven by the engine.

Free play - The amount that the steering wheel can move without moving the front wheels. The maximum allowable amount of free play is less than 2 inches for a parallelogram-type steering system, and 3/8 inch for a rack and pinion steering system.

Frequency - The number of times a complete motion cycle takes place during a period of time (usually measured in seconds).

Friction - The resistance to sliding of two bodies in contact with each other.

Friction ball joint - Outer suspension pivot that does not support the weight of the vehicle. Also called a *follower ball joint.*

Front steer - A construction design of a vehicle that places the steering gear and steering linkage in front of the centerline of the front wheels. Also called *forward steer.*

FWD - Front-wheel drive.

Galvanized steel - Steel with a zinc coating to help protect it from rust and corrosion.

Garter spring - A spring used in a seal to help keep the lip of the seal in contact with the moving part.

Gland nut - The name commonly used to describe the large nut at the top of a MacPherson strut housing. This gland nut must be removed to replace a strut cartridge.

Grease cap - A functional metal cap that keeps grease in and dirt out of wheel bearings. Also called a *dust cap*.

Grease retainer - *See* Grease seal.

Grease seal - A seal used to prevent grease from escaping and to prevent dirt and moisture from entering.

Green tire - An uncured assembled tire. After the green tire is placed in a mold under heat and pressure, the rubber changes chemically and comes out of the mold formed and cured.

Grommet - An eyelet (usually made from rubber) used to protect, strengthen or insulate around a hole or passage.

GVW - Gross vehicle weight. GVW is the weight of the vehicle plus the weight of all passengers and cargo up to the limit specified by the manufacturer.

Half shaft - Drive axles on a front-wheel-drive vehicle or from a stationary differential to the drive wheels.

Halogenated compounds - Chemicals containing chlorine, fluorine, bromine or iodine. These chemicals are generally considered to be hazardous, and any product containing these chemicals should be disposed of using approved procedures.

Haltenberger linkage - A type of steering linkage commonly used on light trucks.

Hanger bearing - See Center support bearing.

HD - Heavy duty.

Helper springs - Auxiliary or extra springs used in addition to the vehicle's original springs to restore proper ride height or to increase the load-carrying capacity of the vehicle.

Hertz - A unit of measurement of frequency. One Hertz is one cycle per second, abbreviated Hz. Named for Heinrich R. Hertz, a nineteenth-century German physicist.

Hooke's Law - The force characteristics of a spring discovered by Robert Hooke (1635-1703), an English physicist. Hooke's Law states that "the deflection (movement or deformation) of a spring is directly proportional to the applied force."

HSS - High-strength steel. A low-carbon alloy steel that uses various amounts of silicon, phosphorus and manganese.

Hub cap - A functional and decorative cover over the lug nut portion of the wheel. *Also see* Wheel cover.

Hydrophilic - A term used to describe a type of rubber used in many all-season tires where the rubber has an affinity for water (rather than repelling it).

Hydrophobic - A term used to describe the repelling of water.

Hydroplaning - Condition that occurs when driving too fast on wet roads. The water on the road gets trapped between the tire and the road, forcing the tire onto a layer of water and off the road surface. All traction between the tire and the road is lost.

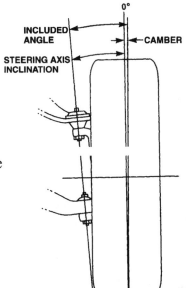

Included angle - SAI angle added to the camber angle of the same wheel.

Independent suspension - A suspension system that allows a wheel to move up and down without undue effect on the opposite side.

Iron - Refined metal from iron ore (ferrous oxide) in a furnace. *Also see* Steel.

IRS - Independent rear suspension.

ISO - International Standards Organization.

Isolator bushing - Rubber bushing used between the frame and the stabilizer bar. Also known as a *stabilizer bar bushing.*

Jounce - Used to describe up-and-down movement.

Jounce bumper - A rubber or urethane stop to limit upward suspension travel. Also called a *bump stop, strikeout bumper, suspension bumper* or *compression bumper.*

Kerf - Large water grooves in the tread of a tire.

King pin - A pivot pin commonly used on solid axles or early model twin I-beam axles that rotate in bushings and allow the front wheels to rotate. The knuckle pivots about the king pin.

King pin inclination - Inclining the tops of the king pins toward each other creates a force stabilizing to the vehicle.

KPI - King pin inclination (also known as *steering axis inclination,* SAI). The angle formed between true vertical and a line drawn between the upper and lower pivot points of the spindle.

Ladder frame - A steel frame for a vehicle that uses cross braces along the length, similar to the rungs of a ladder.

Lateral runout - A measure of the amount a tire or wheel is moving side to side while being rotated. Excessive lateral runout can cause a shimmy-type vibration if the wheels are on the front axle.

Lead - A mild pull that does not cause a force on the steering wheel that the driver must counteract (also known as *drift*).

Leaf spring - A spring made of several pieces of flat spring steel.

Live axle - A solid axle used on the drive wheels; it contains the drive axles that propel the vehicle.

Load index - An abbreviated method that uses a number to indicate the load-carrying capabilities of a tire.

Load-carrying ball joint - Used in a suspension system to provide support and control, and through which the weight (load) of the vehicle is transferred to the frame.

LOBRO joint - A brand name of CV joint.

Lock nut - *See* Prevailing torque nut.

LSD - An abbreviation commonly used for limited slip differentials.

LT - Light truck.

M & S - Mud and snow.

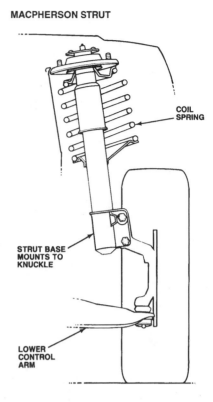

MACPHERSON STRUT

COIL
SPRING

STRUT BASE
MOUNTS TO
KNUCKLE

LOWER
CONTROL
ARM

MacPherson strut - A type of front suspension with the shock absorber and coil spring in one unit, which rotates when the wheels are turned. Assembly mounts to the vehicle body at the top and to one ball joint and control arm at the lower end. It is named for its inventor, Earle S. MacPherson.

Match mount - The process of mounting a tire on a wheel and aligning the valve stem with a mark on the tire. The mark on the tire represents the high point of the tire; the valve stem location represents the smallest diameter of the wheel.

Memory steer - A lead or pull of a vehicle caused by faults in the steering or suspension system. If after making a turn, the vehicle tends to pull in the same direction as the last turn, then the vehicle has memory steer.

Minutes - A unit of measure of an angle. Sixty minutes equal one degree.

Moly grease - Grease containing molybdenum disulfide.

Morning sickness - A slang term used to describe temporary loss of power steering assist when cold caused by wear in the control valve area of a power rack and pinion unit.

MSDS - Material safety data sheets.

NHTSA - Abbreviation for the National Highway Traffic Safety Administration.

NLGI - National Lubricating Grease Institute. Usually associated with grease. The higher the NLGI number, the firmer the grease. #000 is very fluid, whereas #5 is very firm. The consistency most recommended is NLGI #2 (soft).

Noise - Noise is the vibration of air caused by a body in motion.

NVH - Abbreviation for noise, vibration and harshness.

OE - Original equipment.

OEM - Original equipment manufacturer.

Offset - The distance the center section (mounting pad) is offset from the centerline of the wheel.

Orbital steer - *See* Bump steer.

Overcenter adjustment - An adjustment made to a steering gear while the steering is turned through its center straight-ahead position. Also known as a *sector lash adjustment.*

Overinflation - Used to describe a tire with too much tire pressure (greater than maximum allowable pressure).

Oversteer - A term used to describe the handling of a vehicle where the driver must move the steering wheel in the opposite direction from normal while turning a corner. Oversteer handling is very dangerous. Most vehicle manufacturers design their vehicles to understeer rather than oversteer.

Oz-in. - Measurement of imbalance. 3 oz-in. means that an object is out of balance; it would require a 1 oz weight placed 3 inches from the center of the rotating object or a 3 oz weight placed 1 in. from the center or any other combination that when multiplied equals 3 oz-in.

Panhard rod - A horizontal steel rod or bar attached to the rear axle housing at one end and the frame at the other to keep the center of the body directly above the center of the rear axle during cornering and suspension motions. Also called a *track rod.*

Parallelogram - A geometric box shape where opposite sides are parallel (equal distance apart). A type of steering linkage used with a conventional steering gear that uses a pitman arm, center link, idler arm and tie rods.

Penetration - A test for grease where the depth of a standard cone is dropped into a grease sample and its depth is measured.

Perimeter frame - A steel structure for a vehicle that supports the body of the vehicle under the sides, as well as the front and rear.

Pickle fork - A tapered fork used to separate chassis parts that are held together by a nut and a taper. Hitting the end of the pickle fork forces the wedge portion of the tool between the parts to be separated and "breaks the taper." A pickle fork tool is generally *not* recommended because the tool can tear or rip the grease boot of the part being separated.

Pitch - The pitch of a threaded fastener refers to the number of threads per inch.

Pitman arm A short lever arm that is splined to the steering gear cross shaft. It transmits the steering force from the cross shaft to the steering linkage.

Pitman shaft - *See* Sector shaft.

Platform - The platform of a vehicle includes the basic structure (frame and/or major body panels), as well as the basic steering and suspension components. One platform may be the basis for several different brand vehicles.

Pound foot - A measurement of torque. A 1-pound pull, 1 foot from the center of an object.

PPM - Parts per million.

Prevailing torque nut - A special design of nut fastener that is deformed slightly or has other properties that permit the nut to remain attached to the fastener without loosening.

PSI - Pounds per square inch.

Pull - Vehicle tends to go left or right while traveling on a straight, level road.

Rack and pinion - A type of lightweight steering unit that connects the front wheels through tie rods to the end of a long shaft called a *rack*. When the driver moves the steering wheel, the force is transferred to the rack and pinion assembly. Inside the rack housing is a small pinion gear that meshes with gear teeth, which are cut into the rack.

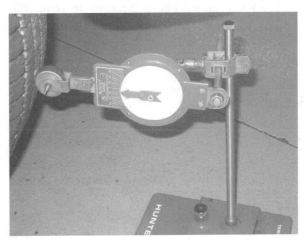

Radial runout - A measure of the amount a tire or wheel is out of round. Excessive radial runout can cause a tramp-type vibration.

Radial tire - A tire whose carcass plies run straight across (or almost straight across) from bead to bead.

Radius rod - A suspension component to control longitudinal (front-to-back) support; it is usually attached with rubber bushings to the frame at one end and the axle or control arm at the other end. *Also see* Strut rod.

Rag joint - *See* Flexible coupling.

Ratio - The expression for proportion. For example, in a typical rear axle assembly, the drive shaft rotates three times faster than the rear axles. It is expressed as a ratio of 3:1 and read as "three to one." Power train ratios are always expressed as driving divided by driven gears.

RBS - Rubber bonded socket.

Rear spacing - *See* Back spacing.

Rear steer - A construction design of a vehicle that places the steering gear and steering linkage behind the centerline of the front wheels.

Rebuilt - *See* Remanufactured.

Remanufactured - A term used to describe a process where a component is disassembled, cleaned, inspected and re-assembled using new or reconditioned parts. According to the Automotive Parts Rebuilders Association (APRA), this same procedure is also called *rebuilt*.

Road crown - A roadway where the center is higher than the outside edges. Road crown is designed into many roads to drain water off the road surface.

Roll bar - *See* Stabilizer bar.

Roll steer - *See* Bump steer.

Run-flat tires - Tires specially designed to operate for reasonable distances and speeds without air inside to support the weight of the vehicle. Run-flat tires usually require the use of special rims designed to prevent the flat tire from coming off the wheel.

RWD - Rear-wheel drive.

SAE - Society of Automotive Engineers.

Saginaw - Brand name of steering components manufactured in Saginaw, Michigan, USA.

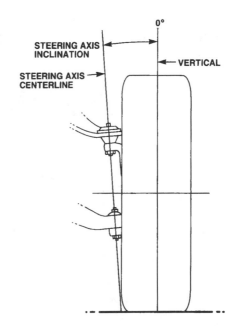

SAI - Steering axis inclination (same as KPI).

Schrader valve - A type of valve used in tires, air-conditioning, and fuel injection systems. Invented in 1844 by August Schrader.

Scrub radius - Refers to where an imaginary line drawn through the steering axis intersects the ground compared to the centerline of the tire. *Zero* scrub radius means the line intersects at the center line of the tire. *Positive* scrub radius means that the line intersects below the road surface. *Negative* scrub radius means the line intersects above the road surface. It is also called *steering offset* by some vehicle manufacturers.

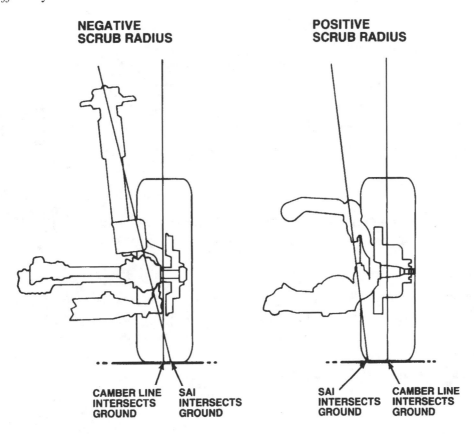

Sector lash - Refers to clearance (lash) between a section of gear (sector) on the pitman shaft in a steering gear. *Also see* Overcenter adjustment.

Sector shaft - The output shaft of a conventional steering gear. It is a part of the sector shaft in a section of a gear that meshes with the worm gear and is rotated by the driver when the steering wheel is turned. It is also called a *pitman shaft.*

SEMA - Specialty Equipment Manufacturers Association.

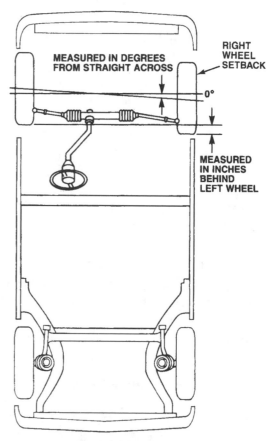

Setback - The amount the front wheels are set back from true parallel with the rear wheels. Positive setback means the right front wheel is set back farther than the left. Setback can be measured as an angle formed by a line perpendicular (90°) to the front axles.

Shackle - A mounting that allows the end of a leaf spring to move forward and backward as the spring moves up and down during normal operation of the suspension.

Shim - A thin metal spacer.

Shimmy - A vibration that results in a rapid back-and-forth motion of the steering wheel. A bent wheel or a wheel assembly that is not correctly balanced dynamically is a common cause of shimmy.

Short/long arm suspension - Abbreviated SLA. A suspension system with a short upper control arm and a long lower control arm. The wheel changes very little in camber with a vertical deflection. Also called *double-wishbone-type suspension.*

Sipes - Small traction-improving slits in the tread of a tire.

SLA - Abbreviation for short/long arm suspension.

Slip angle - The angle between the true centerline of the tire and the actual path followed by the tire while turning.

Solid axle - A solid supporting axle for both front or both rear wheels. Also referred to as a straight axle or nonindependent axle.

Space-frame construction - A type of vehicle construction that uses the structure of the body to support the engine and drive train, as well as the steering and suspension. The outside body panels are nonstructure.

Spalling - A term used to describe a type of mechanical failure caused by metal fatigue. Metal cracks then break out into small chips, slabs or scales of metal. This process of breaking up is called spalling.

Spider - Center part of a wheel. Also known as the *center section.*

Spindle nut - Nut used to retain and adjust the bearing clearance of the hub to the spindle.

Sprung weight - The weight of a vehicle that is supported by the suspension.

Stabilizer bar - A hardened steel bar connected to the frame and both lower control arms to prevent excessive body roll. Also called an *anti-sway* or *anti-roll bar.*

Stabilizer links - Usually consists of a bolt, spacer and nut to connect (link) the end of the stabilizer bar to the lower control arm.

Steady bearing - *See* Center support bearing.

Steel - Refined iron metal with most of the carbon removed.

Steering arms - Arms bolted to or forged as a part of the steering knuckles. They transmit the steering force from the tie rods to the knuckles, causing the wheels to pivot.

Steering coupling disc - *See* Flexible coupling.

Steering gear - Gears on the end of the steering column that multiply the driver's force to turn the front wheels.

Steering knuckle - The inner portion of the spindle that pivots on the king pin or ball joints.

Steering offset - *See* Scrub radius.

Straight axle - *See* Solid axle.

Strikeout bumper - *See* Jounce bumper.

Strut rod - Suspension member used to control forward/backward support to the control arms. Also called *tension* or *compression rod* (TC rod) or *drag rod.*

Strut rod bushing - A rubber component used to insulate the attachment of the strut rod to the frame on the body of the vehicle.

Stud - A short rod with threads on both ends.

Suspension - Parts or linkages by which the wheels are attached to the frame or body of a vehicle. These parts or linkages support the vehicle and keep the wheels in proper alignment.
Suspension bumper - *See* Jounce bumper.

Sway bar - Shortened name for anti-sway bar. *See* Stabilizer bar.

TC rod - *See* Strut rod.

Tension rod - *See* Strut rod.

Thrust angle - The angle between the geometric centerline of the vehicle and the thrust line.

Thrust line - The direction the rear wheels are pointed as determined by the rear wheel toe.

Tie rod - A rod connecting the steering arms together.

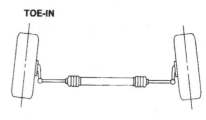

Toe-in - The difference in measurement between the front of the wheels and the back of the wheels (the front are closer than the back).

Toe-out - The back of the tires are closer than the front.

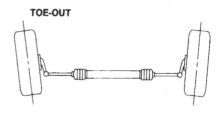

Torque - A twisting force that may or may not result in motion. Measured in lb-ft or Newton-meters.

Torque steer - Torque steer occurs in front-wheel-drive vehicles when engine torque causes a front wheel to change its angle (toe) from straight ahead. The resulting pulling effect of the vehicle is most noticeable during rapid acceleration, especially whenever upshifting of the transmission creates a sudden change in torque.

Torsion bar - A type of spring in the shape of a straight bar. One end is attached to the frame of the vehicle, and the opposite end is attached to a control arm of the suspension. When the wheels hit a bump, the bar twists and then untwists.

Torx - A type of fastener which features a star-shaped indentation for a tool. A registered trademark of the Camcar Division of Textron.

Total toe - The total (combined) toe of both wheels, either front or rear.

Track - The distance between the centerline of the wheels as viewed from the front or rear.

Track rod - A horizontal steel rod or bar attached to rear axle housing at one end and the frame at the other to keep the center of the rear axle centered on the body. Also known as a *panhard rod*.

Tracking - Used to describe the fact that the rear wheels should track directly behind the front wheels.

Tramp - A vibration usually caused by up-and-down motion of an out-of-balance or out-of-round wheel assembly.

Turning radius - Refers to the angle of the steering knuckles that allow the inside wheel to turn at a sharper angle than the outside wheel whenever turning a corner. Also known as toe-out on turns (TOOT) or the Ackerman angle.

UNC - Unified national coarse.

Underinflation - A term used to describe a tire with too little tire pressure (less than minimum allowable pressure).

Understeer - A term used to describe the handling of a vehicle where the driver must turn the steering wheel more and more while turning a corner.

UNF - Unified national fine.

Unit body - A type of vehicle construction first used by the Budd Company of Troy, Michigan, that does not use a separate frame. The body is built strong enough to support the engine and the power train, as well as the suspension and steering system. The outside body panels are part of the structure. *Also see* Space frame construction.

Unsprung weight - The parts of a vehicle not supported by the suspension system. Examples of items that are typical unsprung weight include wheels, tires, and brakes.

Vibration - An oscillation, shake or movement that alternates in opposite directions.

VOC - Volatile organic compounds.

Vulcanization - A process where heat and pressure combine to change the chemistry of rubber.

Wander - A type of handling, which requires constant steering wheel correction to keep the vehicle going straight.

Watt's link - A type of track rod, which uses two horizontal rods pivoting at the center of the rear axle.

Wear bars - *See* Wear indicators.

Wear indicators - Bald area across the tread of a tire when 2/32" or less of tread depth remains.

Wear indicator ball joint - A ball joint design with a raised area around the grease fitting. If the raised area is flush or recessed with the surrounding area of the ball joint, the joint is worn and must be replaced.

Weight-carrying ball joint - *See* Load-carrying ball joint.

Wheel cover - A functional and decorative cover over the entire wheel. *Also see* Hub cap.

Wheelbase - The distance between the centerline of the two wheels as viewed from the side.

Wishbone suspension - *See* Short/long arm suspension.

W/O - Without.

Worm and roller - A steering gear that uses a worm gear on the steering shaft. A roller on one end of the cross shaft engages the worm.

Worm and sector - A steering gear that uses a worm gear that engages a sector gear on the cross shaft.

Zerk - A name commonly used for a grease fitting. Named for its developer, Oscar U. Zerk, in 1922, an employee of the Alemite Corporation. Besides a Zerk fitting, a grease fitting is also called an *Alemite fitting*.

A4 Spanish-Language Glossary

Ackerman principle - principio Ackerman. El ángulo de los brazos de dirección hace que la rueda interior se gire más agudo que la rueda exterior cuando se dobla. Resulta en la divergencia al doblar *[toe-out on turns (TOOT)]*.

Alemite fitting - *Véase* Zerk.

Anti-dive - anti-cabeceo. Palabra que describe la geometría de la suspensión, la cual controla el movimiento del automóvil al frenar.

Anti-squat - anti-deslizamiento. Describe la geometría de la suspensión que controla el movimiento de la carrocería durante la aceleración. La carrocería que se mantiene nivelada tiene 100% antiagacho. Menos que 100% indica que la carrocería se desliza o se baja el trasero durante la aceleración.

Anti-sway bar - *Véase* stabilizer bar.

Articulation test - prueba de articulación. Prueba que exigen algunos fabricantes automóviles para poner a prueba la cantidad de fuerza necesaria para mover el extremo interior de la barra de acomplamiento en el cojinete esférico. La norma usual para esta prueba es entre una libra (0.5 kilos) y seis libras (2.7 kilos) de fuerza.

ASE (National Institute for Automotive Service Excellence) - Instituto Nacional de Excellencia de Servicio Automotriz.

Aspect ratio - alargamiento/relación de envergadura. Relación entre la altura y la anchura de una llanta. Una llanta que tiene un alargamiento de 60 (una llanta serie 60) tiene una altura (del aro de la llanta a la banda de rodamiento) de 60% de la anchura de la sección de corte.

Axial - axial. Alineado con el eje o la línea central de un componente. Desplazamiento axial en una junta esférica quiere decir que hay flojedad en el mismo eje que tiene el espárrago de la junta esférica.

Back spacing - retroceso. Distancia entre el borde posterior de la llanta y el centro de la almohadilla de montaje de la llanta.

Backside setting - regulación trasera - *Ver* espaciamiento trasero.

Ball socket assembly - montaje de rótula. Montaje del brazo terminal de dirección interior que contiene una rótula/articulación esférica donde el montaje se enrosca al extremo de la cremallera de la dirección de piñón y cremallera.

Bolt circle - círculo de pernos. Diámetro (en pulgadas o milímetros) de un círculo que se traza por los centros de los agujeros para pernos de una rueda.

Bounce test - prueba de salto. Prueba que se usa para averiguar la condición de los amortiguadores.

Breather tube - tubo de ventilación. Tubo que conecta los fuelles izquierdos y derechos de un mecanismo de dirección por cremallera.

Brinelling - brinelling. Falla mecánica que describe una abolladura en metal, por ejemplo, la que ocurre cuando se aplica una carga a choque a un balero/cojinete. Llamado en honor de Johann A. Brinell, ingeniero sueco.

Bump steer - salto de dirección. Frase que describe lo que pasa cuando las articulaciones de dirección no están niveladas y hacen que las llantas delanteras se giren o adentro o afuera cuando la suspensión se mueve hacia arriba y hacia abajo. También se llama *orbital steer*.

Bump stop - *Véase* jounce bumper.

Camber - camber. Inclinación de las ruedas hacia adentro o hacia afuera de vertical verdadero.

Cardan joint - junta cardán. Una clase de articulación universal que lleva el nombre de un matemático italiano del siglo dieciseis.

Caster - ángulo de avance. Inclinación hacia adelante o hacia atrás de una línea imaginaria trazada por el eje de dirección vista por el lado del automóvil.

Caster sweep - cálculo del ángulo de cáster o de avance de las ruedas. Proceso que se emplea para medir el ángulo de avance durante el alineamiento de las ruedas en que las ruedas delanteras se giran primeramente hacia dentro, luego hacia afuera, una cantidad especificada.

Center bolt - perno central/capuchino/de centraje. Perno que mantiene unidas en el centro las hojas de un elástico de hojas. También se llama *centering pin (perno centralizador)*.

Center support bearing - balero de soporte central. Balero que soporta el centro de un flecha de cardán larga/eje propulsor largo de un automóvil de propulsión trasera. También se llama *steady bearing* o *hanger bearing*.

Centering pin - perno de centrar - *Ver* Seguro central.

Centerline steering - dirección de la línea central/eje. Palabra que describe la posición del volante de dirección cuando se está manejando en un camino nivelado y recto. El volante debe estar centrado entre tres grados negativos y tres grados positivos, como especifican muchos fabricantes de vehículos.

Chassis - chasis. El bastidor, la suspensión, la dirección y la maquinaria de un automóvil.

Coefficient of friction - coeficiente de fricción. Medida de fricción, normalmente en incrementos de 0 a 1. Un número bajo (0.3) indica una fricción baja y una alta (0.9) una fricción alta.

Coil spring - resorte/muelle espiral. Acero resorte/para muelles en forma de espiral; se usa en los sistemas de suspensión traseros y delanteros.

Compensation - compensación. Proceso que se emplea durante el alineamiento de ruedas en que calibran los sensores para eliminar errores en las indicaciones de alineamiento que pueden ser resultados de una rueda torcida o instalación desigual del sensor en la rueda del vehículo.

Composite - mixto. Describe la combinación de varias partes individuales en un componente mayor. Por ejemplo, una hoja mixta de ballesta se construye de fibra de vidrio y epoxía y un cilindro maestro mixto tiene componentes ambos plásticos (recipiente) y metales (cuerpo de cilíndro).

Compression bumper - *Véase* jounce bumper.

Compression rod - *Véase* strut rod.

Cone - cono. El anillo de rodamiento interior de un cojinete.

Constant velocity joint - junta homocinética/acoplación de velocidad constante. Comúnmente se llaman *CV joints.* Acoplaciones CV son juntas del tren de potencia que pueden transmitir el poder del motor por ángulos grandes sin cambiar la velocidad, como se ve con juntas universales convencionales tipo cardán.

Cotter key - pasador hendido/chaveta. Lazo de metal que se usa para retener tuercas almenadas por instalarlo por un hueco. El tamaño se mide por diámetro y largura (por ejemplo la octava parte de una pulgada por 1.5 pulgadas). También se llama *cotter pin (clavija)*. El nombre viene del verbo del antiguo inglés que quiere decir «cerrar» o «aborchar».

Coupling disc - *Véase* flexible coupling.

Cow catcher - sistema "cow-catcher" o asiento de muelle con dispositivo de protección del neumático. Asiento de bobinas grande que se usa en muchas unidades de puntales MacPherson de General Motors. Si se rompe el resorte, the "cow catcher" impide que el extremo de la bobina se vaya afuera y haga daño a la llanta.

Cross camber/caster - diferencia del ángulo de caída de las ruedas o de cámber/de avance de las ruedas o de cáster. Diferencia de ángulo de un lado del vehículo al otro. La mayoría de los fabricantes recomiendan una diferencia máxima de lado a lado de un medio grado para camber y caster.

Cross steer - sistema de articulación de la dirección "cross-steer". Varillaje de dirección que normalmente se usa para camiones ligeras y regulares.

Cup - copa. El anillo exterior de un balero.

CV (constant velocity) joints - acoplaciones CV. Juntas homocinéticas/acoplación de velocidad constante.

Differential - diferencial. Conjunto mecánico que contiene engranajes que provee desmultiplicación de engranajes y un cambio de dirección de poder del motor y también que permite que las ruedas de propulsión giran a velocidades distintas, como se requiere para doblar la esquina.

Directional stability - estabilidad direccional. Habilidad de un vehículo de seguir derecho con un mínimo de control del conductor. Los vientos de costado e irregularidades del camino no van a tener mucho efecto si la estabilidad direccional es buena.

Dog tracking - vehículo que avanza de lado/fuera de centro. Término que describe el hecho de que las ruedas traseras no siguen directamente detrás de las ruedas delanteras; llamado por la manera en que corren los perros, con las patas traseras fuera de centro para que no se peguen las patas delanteras.

DOT (Department of Transportation) - Abreviatura para el Departamento de Transportación.

Double Cardan - cardán doble. Junta universal que consta de dos articulaciones/juntas cardanes, dejando que la junta alcance mayores ángulos.

Drag link - biela/barra de dirección/acoplación. Describe una varilla en el centro del varillaje de dirección, normalmente se llama *center link (varilla/barra central)*.

Drag rod - *Véase* strut rod.

Drift - deriva. Ligera desviación que no causa una fuerza en el volante que el conductor tenga que contrarrestar (también se llama *lead*). También refiere a una herramienta cónica que se usa para centrar un componente en el agujero de perno antes de meter el perno.

Dropping point - punto de goteo. Temperatura de una grasa cuando se convierte de semi-sólido en líquido bajo condiciones especificadas por ASTM.

Dry park test - prueba de la dirección y/o los componentes de la suspensión. Con las ruedas in hacia adelante y el vehículo en tierra plana, se gira el volante mientras se inspeccionan los componentes de la dirección y la suspensión para flojera.

Durometer - durometro. Tasación/valuación de la dureza de productos de caucho/goma llamado por un instrumento que se use para medir dureza que se desarolló en los 1890.

Dust cap - capuchón. Una tapa de metal que no deja que la grasa salga y que no permite que el polvo entre en los cojinetes de rueda. También se llama *grease cap*.

Flexible coupling - acoplamiento elástico. Parte del mecanismo de dirección entre la columna de dirección y el mecanismo de dirección o conjunto de piñón y cremallera. También se llama *rag joint* o *steering coupling disc*. El acoplamiento elástico sirve para impedir la transmisión al volante de ruido, vibración y fricción del camino y de la dirección.

Flow control valve - vávula de control de flujo. Válvula que controla y reglamenta el flujo de los fluidos de la bomba de la dirección hidráulica al mecanismo de dirección o conjunto de piñón y cremallera. La válvula de control de flujo normalmente es parte del conjunto de la bomba de la dirección hidráulica.

Follower ball joint - Articulación de cardán que se usa en un sistema de suspensión para soportar y controlar sin que el peso del vehículo o la acción de las bobina se traslada por la articulación misma. También se llama *friction ball joint*.

Forward steer - *Véase* front steer.

4 X 2 - Término usado para describir un vehículo pesado de tracción a dos ruedas. El "4" indica el número de ruedas del vehículo y el "2" indica el número de ruedas impulsadas por el motor.

4 X 4 - Término usado para describir un vehículo de tracción a las cuatro ruedas. El primer "4" indica el número de ruedas del vehículo y el segundo "4" indica el número de ruedas impulsadas por el motor.

Free play - juego libre. Distancia que mueve el volante sin mover las ruedas delanteras. La cantidad máxima de juego libre que se permite es menos que 2 pulgadas para un sistema de volante tipo paralelogramo y 3/8 pulgada para un sistema de piñón y cremallera.

Frequency - frequencia. Número de veces una onda se repite en un segundo, que se mide en Hertz (Hz), en una banda.

Friction - fricción. Resistencia al deslizamiento entre dos objetos en contacto.

Friction ball joint - articulación en rótula de fricción. Eje de articulación exterior que no soporta el peso del vehículo. También se llama *follower ball joint.*

Front steer - dirección delantera. Díseño de vehículo en que se encuentran el mecanismo de dirección y las articulaciones de dirección en frente del eje de las ruedas delanteras. También se llama *forward steer.*

FWD (four-wheel drive) - transmisión en las ruedas delanteras.

Galvanized steel - acero galvanizado. Acero con una mano de zinc para proteger el acero de la oxidación y la corrosión.

Garter spring - muelle/bobina toroidal. Resorte usado en un cierre para ayudar mantener el labio del sello en el contacto con la parte móvil.

Gland nut - tuerca de empaque. Nombre que se use comúnmente para describir la tuerca grande a la cabeza de la caja de puntal de MacPherson. Esta tuerca del casquillo se debe quitar para reemplazar el cartucho de puntal.

Grease cap - tapa de engrase. Tapa funcional de metal que no deja que la grasa salga ni que el polvo entre en los cojinetes de rueda. También se llama *dust cap.*

Grease retainer - Retenedor de grasa - *Ver* sello o retén de grasa.

Grease seal - sello de engrase. Sello que se usa para prevenir que el engrase escape y para prevenir que polvo y humedad entren.

Green tire - Neumático verde - Un neumático que no ha sido curado. Después de que el neumático verde ha sido colocado en un molde a cierta temperatura y presión, la goma sufre una transformación química y el neumático sale del molde curado.

Grommet - arandela. Un ojete generalmente hecho de caucho que se usa para proteger, reforzar o aislar alrededor de un hoyo o pasaje.

GVW (gross vehicle weight) - Abreviatura para el peso bruto de vehículo. GVW es el peso del vehículo más el peso de todos pasajeros y la carga hasta el límite especificado por el fabricante.

Half shaft - medio eje. Eje de mando de un vehículo de tracción delantera o un eje que se ubica entre un diferencial estacionario y las ruedas de propulsión.

Halogenated compounds - compuestos halogenados. Sustancias químicas que contienen cloro, flúor, bromo o yodo. Estas sustancias químicas generalmente se consideran peligrosas y cualquier producto que las contiene debe ser deshecho según procedimientos aprobados.

Haltenberger linkage - articulación Haltenberger. Tipo de articulación de dirección normalmente usado en algunos camiones ligeros.

Hanger bearing - *Véase* center support bearing.

HD (heavy duty) - servicio pesado.

Helper springs - ballestas auxiliares. Resortes auxiliares o extras que se usan además de los resortes originales del vehículo para restaurar la altura correcta del chasis o para aumentar la capacidad de carga del vehículo.

Hertz - hertz. Unidad de la medida de la frecuencia, abreviada Hz. Un Hertz es un ciclo por segundo. Llamado en honor de Heinrich R. Hertz, físico alemán del siglo diecinueve.

Hooke's Law - ley de Hooke. Características de la fuerza de un resorte descubiertas por Robert Hooke (1635–1703), físico inglés. La ley de Hooke dice que «la deflection (el movimiento o la deformación) de un resorte es directamente proporcional a la fuerza aplicada».

HSS (high strength steel) - acero de alta resistencia, un acero de aleación bajo en carbono que lleva varias cantidades de silicio, fósforo y manganeso.

Hub cap - tapa de rueda. Cubierta funcional y decorativa sobre la parte de la rueda que lleve las tuerca de rueda. Véase también *wheel cover*.

Hydrophilic - hidrofílico. Término que se usa para describir un tipo de caucho usado en muchas llantas para todas temporadas que tiene una afinidad para el agua (en vez de repelerlo).

Hydrophobic - hidrofóbico. Término que se para describir el repeler del agua.

Hydroplaning - hidroplaneo. Condición que ocurre al manejar demasiado rápido en los caminos mojados donde el agua en el camino se atrapa entre la llanta y el camino, forzando que la llanta esté sobre una cuña de agua y de la superficie del camino. Toda tracción entre la llanta y el camino se pierde.

Included angle - ángulo incluido. Ángulo de SAI que se añade al ángulo cámber de la misma rueda.

Independent suspension - suspensión independiente. Sistema de suspensión que permite que una rueda se mueva hacia arriba y hacia abajo sin efecto indebido en el costado opuesto.

Iron - hierro. Metal refinado de mineral de hierro (óxido ferroso) en un horno. *Véase también* steel.

IRS (independent rear suspension) - cuspensión trasera independiente.

ISO (Internationl Standards Organization) - Organización Internacional de Estándares.

Isolator bushing - buje de caucho que se usa entre el chasis y la barra estabilizadora. También se llama *stabilizer bar bushing (buje de la barra estabilizadora).*

Jounce - rebote o rebotar. Término que se usa para describir el movimiento arriba y abajo. También significa causar el movimiento arriba y abajo.

Jounce bumper - parachoques de rebote. Tope de caucho o uretano para limitar el desplazamiento de la suspensión hacia arriba. También se llama *bump stop, strike-out bumper, suspension bumper o compression bumper.*

Kerf - Cortes - Estrías o surcos de gran tamaño en el ancho de rodada de un neumático.

Kingpin - pivote de dirección. Pasador de pivote que se usa comúnmente en ejes enterizos o en ejes gemelos de viga en I que giran en bujes y dejan que las ruedas anteriores giren. El muñón gira sobre el pivote de dirección.

Kingpin inclination - inclinación del pivote de dirección. Inclinación de las cimas de los pivotes de dirección uno hacia al otro para crear una fuerza estabilizadora al vehículo.

KPI - *Véase* kingpin inclination. También se llama *steering axis inclination (SAI).*

Ladder frame - armazón en escalera. Chasis de acero para un vehículo que usa piezas transversales por su longitud que son parecidas a los escalones de una escalera.

Lateral runout - desviación lateral. Medida del movimiento de una llanta o rueda que se mueve de costado a costado mientras que se gira. Desviación lateral excesivo puede causar una vibración si las ruedas están en el eje delantero.

Lead - derivación. Fuerza ligera que no causa una fuerza en el volante que el conductor tenga que contrarrestar (también se llama *drift*).

Leaf spring - resorte de tipo hoja. Resorte hecho de varios pedazos planos de acero de resorte.

Live axle - eje vivo. Eje enterizo que se usa en las ruedas de propulsión y que lleva los ejes propulsores que propulsan el vehículo.

Load index - índice de carga. Un método abreviado que usa un número para indicar la capacidad de cargar de una llanta.

Load-carrying ball joint - junta de rótula cargadora. Junta de rótula que se usa en el sistema de suspensión para proporcionar soporto y control y por la cual el peso (carga) del vehículo se traslada al chasis.

LÖBRO joint - junta LÖBRO. Marca de una acoplación de velocidad constante.

Lock nut - tuerca de seguridad. *Véase* prevailing torque nut.

LSD (limited slip diferential) - Abreviatura que se usa comúnmente usado para diferencial de deslizamiento limitado.

LT (light truck) - camión ligero.

M & S (mud and snow) - Barro y nieve.

MacPherson strut - puntal MacPherson. Tipo de suspensión anterior con el amortiguador y el resorte espiral en una unidad que gira cuando las ruedas se giran. El conjunto se monta a la carrocería por encima y a la junta de rótula y al brazo de mando en el extremo más bajo. Llamado en honor de su inventor, Earle S. MacPherson.

Match mount - montaje por coincidencia. Proceso de montar un neumático en una rueda y coincidir la cola de la válvula con una marca en la llanta. La marca en la llanta representa el punto más alto de la llanta y la ubicación de la cola de válvula representa el diámetro más pequeño de la rueda.

Memory steer - dirección con memoria. Derivación o esfuerzo de un vehículo causado por defectos en el sistema de dirección o suspensión. Si después de hacer una vuelta el vehículo sigue en la misma dirección como la última vuelta, el vehículo tiene dirección con memoria.

Minutes - minutos. Unidad de medida de un ángulo; 60 minutos igualan 1 grado.

Moly grease - grasa molibdeno. Grasa que contiene disulfido de molibdeno.

Morning sickness - dirección asistida está fría/necesita entrar en calor. Argot que se usa para describir la pérdida temporaria de la asistencia de poder cuando en condiciones frías; causada por desagaste en el área de la válvula de control de una cremallera de dirección hidráulica.

MSDS (material safety data sheets) - hojas de datos de seguridad.

NHTSA (National Highway Traffic Safety Administration) - Abreviatura para la Administración Nacional de Seguridad del Tráfico de Carreteras.

NLGI (National Lubricating Grease Institute) - Instituto Nacional de la Grasa Lubricante. Generalmente asociado con la grasa. Cuanto más alto el numero de NLGI, tanto más firme la grasa: No. 000 es muy líquido mientras que No. 5 es muy firme. La consistencia más recomendada es NLGI No. 2 (suave).

Noise - ruido **-** Ruido es la vibración de aire causada por un cuerpo en movimiento.

NVH (noise, vibration, and friction) - Abreviatura para ruido, vibración y fricción.

OE (original equipment) - equipo original.

OEM (original equipment manufacturer) - fabricante de equipo original.

Offset - descentramiento. Distancia que está desviada la sección central (almohadilla de montaje) del eje de la rueda.

Orbital steer - *Véase* bump steer.

Over-center adjustment - ajuste del mecanismo de dirección (en posición central) Ajuste que se hace a una caja de dirección mientras la conducción se gira por su centro recto adelante con la dirección pasando por su punto medio. También conocido como *sector lash adjustment (ajuste del juego del sector).*

Overinflation - sobreinflación. Término que se usa para describir una llanta con demasiado presión (más que la máxima presión admisible).

Oversteer - sobreviraje. Término que se usa para describir el manejo de un vehículo en que el conductor tiene que mover el volante en la dirección opuesta de normal al doblar la esquina. El sobreviraje es muy peligroso. La mayoría de los fabricantes de vehículos diseñan sus vehículos para insuficiente viraje en vez de sobreviraje.

Oz.-in. - onza pulgada. Medida del desequilibrio: 3 oz.-in. dice que un objeto está desequilibrado tal que require el peso de 1 oz. (onza) colocado a 3 pulgadas del centro del objeto que gira o un peso de 3 oz. 1 pulgada del centro o cualquier otra combinación que cuando se multiplica iguala 3 oz.-in.

Panhard rod - barra Panhard. Barra horizontal de acero fijada por un extremo a la caja del eje trasero y al chasis por el otro para mantener el centro de la carrocería directamente encima del centro del eje trasero durante doblar y movimientos de la suspensión. También se llama *track rod..*

Parallelogram - paralelogramo. Forma geométrica como caja, tal que los lados opuestos son paralelos (a una distancia igual).

Penetration - penetración - Una prueba de ensayo para grasas en la que un cono estándar se deja caer en una muestra de la grasa y la profundidad de la huella causada es medida.

Perimeter frame - armazón perimétrica. Estructura de acero para un vehículo que soporta la carrocería del vehículo debajo de los lados así como la frente y el trasero.

Pickle fork - horquilla en disminución. Horquilla estrechada que se usa para separar las partes del chasis que se mantienen unidas por una tuerca y un cono de mayor a menor. Golpear el fin de la horquilla en disminución hace que la porción de la cuña de la herramienta entre las partes sea separada y deshace la unión en forma de cono. La horquilla en disminución generalmente no se recomienda porque puede romper o puede rasgar la cubierta de lubricante de la parte que se separa.

Pitch - paso de rosca. Paso de rosca de un cierre enhebrado refiere al número de hilos por pulgada.

Pitman shaft - *Véase* sector shaft.

Platform - plataforma. La plataforma de un vehículo incluye la estructura básica (chasis y/o planchas de carrocería mayores) y además los componentes básicos de dirección y suspensión. Una plataforma puede ser la base para varios vehículos de marcas diferentes.

Pound foot - pie-libra - Una medida del par de fuerza: Una fuerza de una libra ejercida a un pie del centro de un objeto.

PPM (parts per million) - partes por millón.

Prevailing torque nut - tuerca dominante de torsión. Tuerca con un diseño especial tal como deformación o que tiene otras propiedades que permiten que la tuerca se queje fijada al fijador sin aflojarse.

PSI (pounds per square inch) - libras por pulgada cuadrada.

Pull - tiro. Refiere a vehículos que tienden a ir a la izquierda o la derecha al viajar en un camino recto y plano.

Rack and pinion - piñón y cremallera. Tipo de unidad de dirección ligera que conecta las ruedas delanteras por una barra de ajuste al extremo de un eje largo que se llama *rack (cremallera)*. Cuando el conductor gira el volante, la fuerza se transfiere al mecanismo de piñón y cremallera dentro de lo cual se encuentra un engranaje pequeño de piñón que engrana con los dientes del engranaje en la cremallera.

Radial runout - desviación radial. Medida de cuánto una llanta o la rueda está ovalada. La desviación radial excesiva puede causar una vibración de tipo barreta.

Radial tire - llanta/neumático radial. Llanta con las capas de carcasa que son perpendiculares o casi perpendiculares a los aros de las llantas.

Radius rod - varilla radial. Componente de suspensión para controlar el soporte en la dirección del movimiento del vehículo o "de adelante a atrás" y generalmente se fija con bujes de caucho al chasis por un extremo y al eje o al brazo de mando en el otro. *Véase también* strut rod.

Rag joint - *Véase* flexible coupling.

Ratio - ratio/tasa/relación. La expresión para la proporción. Por ejemplo, en un conjunto de eje trasero, la flecha cardán gira tres veces más rápida que los ejes traseros, lo que se expresa como una relación de tres a uno. Relaciones en un sistema de motor se expresan dividiendo la rotación del mecanismo motriz por la rotación del mecanismo movido.

RBS (rubber-bonded socket) - casquillo de caucho-metal o caucho-metal.

Rear spacing - *Véease* back spacing.

Rear steer - dirección trasera. Diseño de un vehículo que coloca la caja de dirección y el varillaje de dirección detrás del eje de las ruedas delanteras.

Rebuilt - *Véase* remanufactured.

Remanufactured - reconstruido. Término que se usa para describir un componente que se desmonta, se limpia, se inspecciona y se vuelve a montar utilizando repuestos nuevos o rehabilitados. Según la Automotive Parts Rebuilders Association (APRA), este componente mismo también se llama *rebuilt*.

Road crown - convexidad del camino. Calzada donde el centro es más alto que el exterior. La convexidad del camino se diseña en muchos caminos para desaguar la superficie del camino.

Roll bar - *Véase* stabilizer bar.

Roll steer - *Véase* roll steer.

Run-flat tires - llantas que pueden rodar desinchadas. Llantas especialmente diseñadas para operar a distancias y velocidades razonables sin aire adentro para soportar el peso del vehículo.

RWD (rear-wheel drive) - transmisión por las ruedas traseras.

SAE (Society of Automotive Engineers) - Sociedad de Ingenieros Automotrices.

Saginaw - Marca de componentes de dirección fabricados en Saginaw, Michigan, USA.

SAI (steering axle inclination) - inclinación del eje de dirección (el mismo que KPI).

Schrader valve - válvula schrader. Válvula cargada de resorte que se usa en los puertos de servicio del riel del combustible y el sistema de aire acondicionado. Inventado en 1844 por August Schrader.

Scrub radius - Línea imaginaria dibujada por el eje de dirección y que se cruza el suelo en un punto comparado con el centro de la línea de la llanta. *Zero scrub radius* significa que la línea se cruza el centro de la línea del neumático. *Positive scrub radius* significa que la línea se cruza debajo de la superficie de la carretera y *negative scrub radius* significa que la línea se cruza encima de la superficie de la carretera. También se llama *steering offset* por algunos fabricantes de vehículo.

Sector lash - juego del sector. Espacio libre (juego) entre una sección de engranaje (sector) en el eje pitman en el mecanismo de dirección. *Véase también* over-center adjustment.

SEMA (Specialty Equipment Market Association) - Asociación del Mercado de Equipo Especializado.

Setback - alineación incorrecta de la rueda. Cantidad que las ruedas delanteras son retrasadas de paralela verdadera con las ruedas traseras. La alineación positiva significa que la rueda delantera correcta es más retrasada que la izquierda.

Shackle - grillete. Montaje que permite que el extremo de un resorte de tipo hoja se mueva hacia adelante y hacia atrás mientra que se mueve hacia arriba y hacia abajo durante operación normal de la suspensión.

Shim - lámina de ajuste. Espaciador de metal delgado.

Shimmy - vibración. Vibración que tiene como resultado un movimiento rápido del volante hacia atrás y hacia adelante. Una rueda doblada o una asamblea de rueda que no está equilibrada correctamente son las causas comunes de *shimmy.*

Short/long arm suspension (SLA) - suspensión de brazo corto y largo. Sistema de suspensión con un brazo del control superior corto y un brazo inferior largo. La rueda cambia muy poco en el ángulo cámber con una deflexión vertical.

Sipes - acanaladuras. Ranuras pequeñas en la banda de una llanta que mejoran la tracción.

SLA (short/long arm) - Abreviatura para suspensión de brazo corto y largo. También se llama *double wishbone type suspension.*

Slip angle - ángulo de deslizamiento. Ángulo entre la línea central verdadera de la llanta y el desplazamiento verdadero seguido por la llanta mientras gira.

Solid axle - eje enterizo. Eje (de soporte) de una pieza para las dos ruedas anteriores o las dos ruedas traseras. También se le dice *straight axle* o *nonindependent axle.*

Space-frame construction - carrocería monocasco. Tipo de construcción de vehículo que usa la estructura de la carrocería para soportar el motor y mecanismo de dirección tanto como la conducción y suspensión. Las planchas de carrocería exteriores no son elementos estructurales.

Spalling - decantillado. Término que se usa para describir un tipo de falla mecánica causada por fatiga del metal. El metal agrieta luego estalla en astillas pequeñas, en los trozos o en las escalas de metal.

Spider - araña. Parte central de una rueda; también conocida como *center section (la sección central).*

Spindle nut - tuerca de vástago. Tuerca que se usa para retener y ajustar el espacio libre de cojinete del eje al vástago.

Sprung weight - peso suspendido. Peso de un vehículo sostenido por la suspensión.

Stabilizer bar - barra estabilizadora. Barra de acero endurecido que se conecta al chasis y ambos brazos de mando inferiores para prevenir el balanceo de la carrocería rolido. También se llama *antisway bar (barra contra la osiliación lateral)* o *antiroll bar (barra antirolida)*.

Stabilizer links - eslabón de estabilizador. Cerrojo, espaciador y tuerca que conectan el extremo de la barra estabilizadora al brazo de mando inferior.

Steady bearing - *Véase* center support bearing.

Steel - acero. Metal de hierro refinado con la mayor parte del carbono quitado.

Steering arms - brazos de dirección. Brazos acerrojados a o fraguados como parte de los muñónes de dirección. Transmiten la fuerza de dirección de las barras de ajuste a los muñónes, haciendo que las ruedas giren sobre su eje.

Steering coupling disc - *Véase* flexible coupling.

Steering gear - caja de dirección. Engranajes en el extremo de la columna de dirección que multiplican la fuerza de conductor para girar las ruedas anteriores.

Steering knuckle - muñón de dirección. Parte interior del eje que gira sobre su eje en el pivote de dirección o en las juntas de rótula.

Steering offset - *Véase* scrub radius.

Straight axle - *Véase* solid axle.

Strike-out bumper - *Véase* jounce bumper.

Strut rod - brazo de retención. Componente de la suspensión que se usa para controlar soporte en la dirección de movimiento del vehículo a los brazos de mando. También se llama *tension or compression rod (TC rod)* o *drag rod*.

Strut rod bushing - buje de barra de retención. Componente de caucho que se usa para aislar la fijación de la barra de retención al chasis a la carrocería del vehículo.

Stud - espárrago. Barra corta con hilos en ambos extremos.

Suspension - suspensión. Partes o articulaciones por las cuales las ruedas se sujetan al chasis o a la carrocería de un vehículo. Estas partes o articulaciones soportan el vehículo y mantienen el alineamiento apropiado de las ruedas.

Suspension bumper - tope de suspensión - *Ver* tope de carrera de la suspensión.

Sway bar - barra contra la osilación lateral. Nombre corto para *antisway bar;* véase *stabilizer bar*.

TC rod - *Véase* strut rod.

Tension rod - *Véase* strut rod.

Thrust angle - ángulo del eje trasero en relación con la línea central de vehículo. Ángulo entre la línea central geométrica del vehículo y la línea central.

Thrust line - línea central. Dirección de las ruedas traseras determinada por la convergencia/divergencia de las ruedas traseras.

Tie rod - tirante de acoplamiento de dirección. Barra que conecta los brazos de dirección.

Toe-in - convergencia. Diferencia medida entre la parte anterior de las ruedas y la parte posterior (las frentes de las llantas se acercan más que las partes de atrás).

Toe-out - divergencia. Las partes de atrás de las llantas se acercan más que las frentes.

Torque - torque/torsión. Fuerza que tuerce que se mide en libras pies (lb-ft) o Newton–metros (N–m), que pueda resultar en movimiento.

Torque steer - jaloneo del volante al acelerar al fondo. Este jaloneo ocurre en vehículos de tracción delantera cuando el torque del motor hace que una rueda anterior exhiba convergencia o divergencia. El efecto de tiro de vehículo que resulta se nota mucho durante aceleración rápida, especialmente cuando el cambio de la transmisión de baja a alta velocidad crea un cambio repentino en el torque.

Torsion bar - barra de torsión. Tipo de resorte en la forma de una barra recta; un extremo se conecta al chasis del vehículo y el extremo contrario se conecta a un brazo de mando de la suspensión. Cuando las ruedas se golpean con un choque, la barra tuerce y luego destuerce.

Torx - tipo de cierre que tiene una endedura en forma de estrella para una herramienta. Una marca registrada de la División Camcar de Textron.

Total toe - convergencia total - La combinación de la convergencia de las dos ruedas, delanteras o traseras.

Track - ancho de rodada del vehículo. Distancia entre la línea central de las ruedas como se ve desde la frente o el trasero.

Track rod - barra de acoplamiento de la dirección. Barra horizontal de acero que se fija a la caja del eje trasero en un extremo y al chasis en el otro para mantener el centro del eje trasero centrado en el carrocería. También se llama *panhard rod*.

Tracking - rastrear. Término que se usa para describir el hecho de que las ruedas traseras deben rastrear directamente detrás de las ruedas anteriores.

Tramp - barreta. Vibración generalmente causado por el movimiento hacia arriba y hacia abajo de un conjunto de rueda ovalado o fuera de equilibrio.

Turning radius - radio de giro. Ángulo de los muñones de dirección que permiten que la rueda interior alcance un ángulo más agudo que la rueda exterior cuando dobla la esquina. También se llama *toe-out on turns - TOOT (divergencia)* o *Ackerman angle (ángulo Ackerman)*.

UNC (unified national coarse) - rosca unificada americana normal.

Underinflation - falta de presión/bajo de inflación. Término que se usa para describir una llanta con la presión demasiado baja (menos que la presión admisible mínima).

Understeer - insuficiente viraje. Término que se usa para describir el manejo de un vehículo en que el conductor tiene girar el volante cada vez mas al doblar la esquina.

UNF (unified national fine) - rosca unificada americana fina.

Unit-body - carrocería de una pieza. Tipo de construcción de vehículo, usado primero por la compañía Budd de Troy, Michigan, que no usa una carrocería distinta. La carrocería está construida suficientemente fuerte para soportar el motor y el tren de potencia así como también la suspensión y sistema de dirección. Las planchas de carrocería exteriores forman parte de la estructura. *Véase también* space-frame construction .

Unsprung weight - peso no suspendido. Partes de un vehículo que el sistema de suspensión no soporta. Unos ejemplos típicos son las ruedas, las llantas y los frenos.

Vibration - vibración. Oscilación, sacudida o movimiento que alterna en direcciones opuestas.

VOC (volatile organic compounds) - compuestos orgánicos volátiles.

Vulcanization - vulcanización. Proceso en que calor y presión se combinan para cambiar la química de caucho.

Wander - movimiento anormal de la dirección del vehículo. Tipo de manejo que requiere corrección constante del volante para mantener que el vehículo vaya recto hacia adelante.

Watt's link - conexión de Watt. Tipo de barra de acoplamiento que usa dos barras horizontales girando sobre un eje en el centro del eje trasero.

Wear bars - *Véase* wear indicators.

Wear indicator ball joint - indicador de desgaste del tipo de articulación en rótula. Diseño de junta de rótula con una área levantada alrededor de la conexión de engrase. Si el área levantada es al mismo nivel que o más bajo que el área circundante de la junta de rótula, la junta se está gastada y se debe reemplazar.

Wear indicators - indicadores de desgaste. Zonas desgastadas que aparecen en la banda de una llanta cuando queda sólo 2/32 de una pulgada o menos de profundidad de la banda.

Weight–carrying ball joint - *Véase* load-carrying ball joint.

Wheel cover - cubrerueda. Cubierta funcional y decorativa sobre la rueda entera. *Véasa también* hub cap.

Wheelbase - distancia entre ruedas. Distancia entre la línea central de las dos ruedas como se ve de un lado.

Wishbone suspension - soporte ahorquillado.*Véase* short/long arm suspensions (SLA).

W/O (without) - Sin.

Worm and roller - tornillo sin fin y rodillo. Caja de dirección que usa un engranaje sinfin en el eje de la columna de dirección. Un rodillo en un extremo del eje de cruce engrana el tornillo sin fin.

Worm and sector - dirección por tornillo sinfin y sector. Caja de dirección que usa un engranaje sinfin para engranar el engranaje de sector en el eje de cruce.

Zerk - Zerk. Nombre que se usa comúnmente para una grasera. Llamado en 1922 en honor de su diseñador, Oscar U. Zerk, un empleado de la Corporación Alamite. Una grasera también se llama *Alamite fitting*.

Index